TOOLS

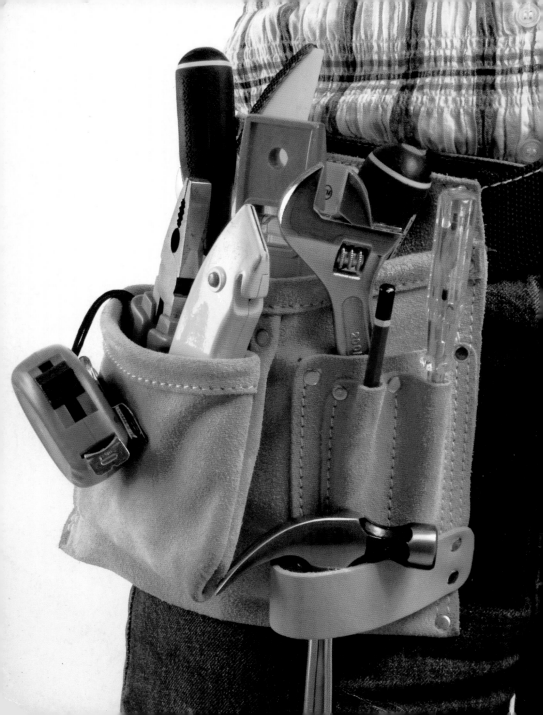

TOOLS

A tool-by-tool guide to choosing and using 150 home essentials

STEVE DODDS

FIREFLY BOOKS

A FIREFLY BOOK

Published by Firefly Books Ltd. 2005

Copyright © Elwin Street Limited 2004

First printing

Publisher Cataloging-in-Publication Data (U.S.)

Dodds, Steve.
   Tools : a tool-by-tool guide to choosing and using 150 home essentials / Steve Dodds. –1st ed.
[224] p. : ill., col. photos., col. ; cm.
Includes index.
Summary: A home and car a guide to building a tool kit and learning how to identify the right tool for the right job.
ISBN 1-55407-060-0 (pbk.)
1. Tools. 2. Tools – Handbooks, manuals, etc.
I. Title.
621.9 22   TJ1195.D63 2005

Library and Archives Canada Cataloguing in Publication

Dodds, Steve
           Tools : a tool-by-tool guide to choosing and using 150 home essentials / Steve Dodds.
Includes index.
ISBN 1-55407-060-0 (pbk.)
1. Tools--Handbooks, manuals, etc. I. Title.
TJ1195.D63 2005   621.9   C2004-905717-0

Published in the United States by
Firefly Books (U.S.) Inc.
P.O. Box 1338, Ellicott Station
Buffalo, New York 14205

Published in Canada by
Firefly Books Ltd.
66 Leek Crescent
Richmond Hill, Ontario L4B 1H1

Conceived and produced by
Elwin Street Limited
79 St John Street
London EC1M 4NR
www.elwinstreet.com

Cover design by Sharanjit Dhol
Internal design by Thomas Keenes
Edited by Diana Steedman

Printed in Singapore

Both hand and power tools can be dangerous. Exercise extreme caution and good safety practice at all times.

All statements, information and advice given is believed to be true and accurate; however, neither the author, copyright holder nor the publisher can accept any legal liability for errors or omissions or any injury caused.

Contents

Introduction

An enormous range of tools has developed over the ages. Some are complex and specialized, while others are exquisitely simple. A bartender, a brain surgeon, an ironworker each uses tools to serve their trade. Although this book does not encompass olive pitters, hemostats or drift pins, it does comprehensively cover a range of tools that you will need to build, improve, maintain and repair your home and belongings, as well as use for your hobbies or pastimes.

In today's information era, people's interaction with their surroundings is more abstract and less hands-on than it was just a few decades ago. Even shopping for groceries and produce can be done from a computer. The desire to reconnect with the physical by making or fixing something, no matter how small, has fueled many to join the do-it-yourself revolution.

Everyone, though, can benefit from understanding how hand and power tools are used, even if their tool kit amounts to only a screwdriver and a hammer in the kitchen drawer. It's the first step towards the ability to tackle a maintenance or improvement job yourself, rather than pay a professional or depend on someone else to do it for you.

Sadly, many people do start at a disadvantage because they have not been taught how to use even the most basic of tools correctly. Those who were fortunate enough to have some instruction on the basics of household tools generally had the knowledge passed down to them by a relative or friend, or learned at school or through trial and error. It's a great way to learn, but Dad or your high school shop teacher might not be an authority on every tool. And even the most grizzled veterans have a few gaps in their knowledge.

So whether you are a beginner or you just want to feel less intimidated by the choices and differences in tools when visiting the hardware store, this book provides a solid reference of information from which to start to understand what tool does what task best and why.

With the huge rise in popularity of DIY work, it's increasingly common for private individuals to pick up where the pros leave off and undertake small-scale construction and renovation projects on their own. If you already have a firm base of skills to work from, *Tools* will help you pick up subtleties, tips and trivia to flesh out your knowledge, and you'll find plenty of information to refer to when it's time to expand your collection of tools.

The resources found in this book can be used by everyone from architects and builders to Jane and Joe DIYer to get cutting-edge information on tools, equipment, materials, cost estimating, market trends and project planning.

Lastly, a few words about the illustrations. The goal is to provide an image that accurately represents a tool or process, not to endorse or recommend any particular brand or specific product. Careful consideration will need to go into choosing the right tool for you, as you'll soon learn. Multinational brands, where possible, are included, but be aware that an individual company's product lines may vary from market to market, and from year to year.

How to use this book

The aim of this book is to be useful even when you don't know what you're looking for. To achieve this, there are several ways to access the information you don't know you want! The book is divided into three sections. The first, Practical Matters, helps you figure out what tools you should own, how or where to buy them, and how to use them safely.

The second section, Tool Kits, provides you with a series of "starter packs" appropriate for different situations and demands. Look at the kits as introductions into the third section, the Tool Guide. If you're a novice, Tool Kits is a good place to start. It's more manageable than diving straight into the Tool Guide as it introduces you to the major purposes of the tools.

The first of the tool kits is simple and will help you establish a very basic set of

tools. The other kits provide guidance when you want or need to expand your collection, as you develop handicraft techniques or acquire high-maintenance property. To conclude the Tool Kits section, there is guidance on how to set up and develop a home workshop.

Here's an example of how you might find yourself using this book.

You have a few pieces of copper pipe to cut. What tool should you use?

Thumb through the Tool Guide under Cutting (page 64) and look in the entry headings for

Some tools appear in more than one kit. This doesn't mean you need to purchase multiples of the same tool. It just serves to show how adding a few items to a most basic tool kit can prepare you to take on a whole range of projects working with different materials and requiring more complex skills.

If you enjoy do-it-yourself projects, you may soon find yourself going beyond the range of tasks suggested. At that point, you're best served by the Tool Guide. Here, the information is organized into nine general categories of tool use:

• Measuring and layout
• Cutting
• Making holes
• Holding and supporting work
• Shaping
• Driving and prying
• Fastening
• Surface preparation
• Storage and protection

Within each category there are individual tool entries, each with an image of the tool, a full description of its function, and at-a-glance reference to:

• Materials that the tool is suitable for
• In which of the tool kits (pages 22 to 39) the tool is included
• Price range
• Level of necessity
• Degree of skill required for its use

There are notes on each of the tool's use, selection and care and, where helpful, a diagram of it in operation. In some cases, descriptions of specialized or more expensive variations are included, as well as further detail and general advice on accessories that will expand a tool's versatility and its capabilities.

"Materials," and seek out metal or piping. There are possible options: for example, a powered miter saw with a special blade (page 88), a hacksaw (page 79), and a tubing cutter (page 72).

After reading each description, you may consider the miter saw is a little expensive and too time-consuming to assemble for your needs; a hacksaw would do the job but with some effort and skill required; a tubing cutter you find is simple to use, inexpensive, and leaves a clean cut every time.

You may then decide to purchase an inexpensive tubing cutter for your tool kit or you may go for borrowing your neighbor's hacksaw.

1 PRACTICAL MATTERS

What tools do I need?

Well, that depends . . . It's an open-ended question, and a lot like asking, "What's the best way to travel from here to over there?" When it comes down to it, tools are simply the means to an end. Consider the tool-buying process as if you were planning a trip.

If all you ever plan to do is run day-to-day errands in your neighborhood, all you really need is a bicycle. It could be a well-tuned machine or a cheap clunker you don't mind abusing and wouldn't miss if it were stolen. Either one would get you to the grocery store and back. But you don't need a $3,000 mountain bike just to pick up some milk, and you don't want to deal with the loose chain and bad brakes on the shabby bike every time you run out of Pop Tarts. Somewhere in between there is a happy medium between economy and excess that is appropriate to you and your requirements.

A basic set of tools works the same way. You don't need to buy a lot of fancy equipment or brand-new top-of-the-line tools if you're using them occasionally for small jobs. But if your first tools are the start of a collection you intend to expand over the years, it's worth spending extra for quality.

It usually makes sense to acquire additional tools one at a time as you need them, or on a project-by-project basis. Most people's tool collections accumulate this way; they buy the tools when they first need them, but are then prepared to tackle a whole new range of jobs.

Sometimes it can make sense to rent rather than to buy. This is especially true when you need an expensive or more specialized piece of equipment you may use just once. The decision is not so clear-cut with less specialized, less costly equipment you may use infrequently. You should compare the cost of renting two or three times with the cost of buying the tool. It may be more cost-effective to buy it the first time around. But don't forget once you own it, you'll have to store it somewhere, which is a key consideration if you live where space is at a premium.

Be it woodworking, metalworking, plumbing, or restoring cars, as you learn more about the techniques and processes of a particular discipline, you'll learn about the tools, materials, and spaces required for each activity. You'll start to acquire tools more specialized to the areas you enjoy and tailor your collection accordingly.

Here are a few questions to consider when developing your collection:

- What tasks do you want to perform?

- How much use do you expect to get from your tools?

- How involved are the projects you want to take on?

- How much do you want to spend?

- How much space do you have?

Answer these questions and you'll have a strategy to guide your purchases now and in the future.

Gaining skill with tools

Continuing Education classes are a good way to learn some basic skills. You may need to provide your own hand tools and materials, but the school will provide access to try larger or more expensive tools. This is especially helpful if you are considering a specific hobby; you can use the tool without making a large investment in equipment. Public schools, community colleges, and some YMCA/YWCAs and home centers offer lessons on particular projects. Look around in your local area.

In most areas, there are local or regional clubs and guilds dedicated to particular interests. There are clubs for people interested in general woodworking and others focus on specific areas like carving or turning. Other organizations focus on automobiles, jewelry making, boating, etc. To find them, search the Internet or ask retailers likely to sell materials or supplies to the membership. Clubs are excellent resources for a novice and plenty of people with similar interests who are happy to help out a beginner.

Persuade a knowledgable and experienced friend to work with you on a project. Just holding the flashlight or fetching the tools is a chance to watch how it's done, ask questions, and learn. Volunteer for work parties at a church or community center or with organizations such as Habitat for Humanity. It's a good opportunity to spend time around a work site and learn a few new things. You may spend the first few visits pushing a broom and moving

materials around, but hey, everyone needs to start somewhere.

Consider working a part-time or summer job, if you're young or retired, to help out a tradesman or work in a maintenance department. At best, you'll pick up some new skills and earn some pocket money. At worst it will convince you to stay in college or remind you why you retired.

Quality versus price

Once you have decided what tools you need and you know how much you want to spend, you're ready to go shopping.

When buying a car, you wouldn't walk into a dealer and say, "I'd like a two-door sedan please," and whip out your checkbook. You'd want to see what was available from competing manufacturers, read some reviews, take a couple for test-drives, and maybe ask an owner or two how they like their cars. This much research is warranted when you're preparing to spend thousands of dollars on a car. You don't need to go to such lengths when you're shopping for tools, but it is helpful to use some of the same steps.

The difference between buying inexpensive hand tools and expensive power tools is the level of risk in making a bad decision. In the grand scheme, screwdrivers all function pretty much the same. However, you can quickly chew up the tips or twist the handles right off cheap screwdrivers, and then you need to spend a few more bucks on another one. If you stick with a recognized brand name, chances are that you will buy a decent product that will help you perform the task more effectively.

First, figure out what features you are looking for and how much you are hoping to spend. Many retailers stock several manufacturers and each manufacturer has variations of the same instrument. The Tool Guide helps you review a tool's features and variations, and to further hone your

choice, look for recent magazine reviews. These reviews generally compare a tool's performance and value and note options or differences that you may otherwise over-look. Often, they will name an "Editor's Choice" or "Best Value" if an item or accessory is especially outstanding and some publications survey their subscribers to name a "Reader's Choice." This is all helpful once you've decided on a few possible alternatives, and you can then visit a store to check them out. If you're left-handed, you may find that the controls and adjustments on one particular model are less awkward than another. Or if you are going to use a cordless drill all day, you may decide giving up some of the power of a larger battery model is worth the weight saving in a smaller brand. Go with the most comfortable tool.

Plan ahead purchasing

- If you are going to need several cordless tools, it's worth researching whether batteries and chargers are inter-changeable between different manufacturers. You may not want an armada of incompatible pieces leaving you constantly checking which charger belongs with which tool.

Where to buy

Whether it is down to your local home center, at an antique market, or on the Web, you will want to look over and check out the goods.

Basic hand tools are available in many stores, but you should generally avoid buying them at the grocery store or pharmacy. If you need a wrench at 2 a.m. on Christmas Eve to assemble a gift, that's probably your only choice. (Though if you create one of the basic tool kits listed in Tool Kits (see pages 22 to 39), you'll already be prepared to build whatever Santa happens to drop down your chimney.) Purchasing tools at your local hardware store or home center is a better alternative. Large chain home centers supply a good selection of the more common tools, though they may not have some of the more unusual items. And the likelihood of obtaining knowledgeable assistance can be haphazard. Hardware stores may have fewer large items, but they're often better sources for hand tools and fasteners and expert advice.

When it comes to expensive hand tools and larger shop tools, you'll want to visit larger hardware stores, tool dealers, and woodworking stores for the best selection. There are national chains and several catalog mail-order companies specializing in fine woodworking tools and equipment.

Buying tools online—especially power tools—is now a mainstream option. It's still a good idea to research the products and check them out in person, and even if you

buy from a traditional vendor, it doesn't hurt to compare online pricing. If you do decide to buy online, verify the seller is a legitimate company, and protect your credit information. Understand any shipping, return or restocking policies and fees and make sure you get what you expected. Be wary of unusually low prices. Sometimes sellers will advertise the basic tool for a reduced price, but charge for accessories usually included in the list price. In other instances, the retailer may be offering reconditioned tools, which are those that were originally faulty and returned to the manufacturer for repair. This isn't always, nor necessarily, a bad thing, because it means the company has thoroughly

checked and bench-tested the tool prior to resale, but you should be aware of this prior to your purchase.

You also can buy used tools. This is a good way to obtain a particular tool for a reduced price, or a higher quality of tool than you would normally afford. Try garage sales, flea markets, and want ads, or a used-tool dealer. Check your local Yellow Pages too. If you decide on this option, familiarize yourself with the tool as new beforehand. It's easier to notice any problems or defects you may encounter, and you'll learn the difference between a

Buying second-hand

Some points to keep in mind when buying used tools:

• Ask why the owner is selling it. The answers may give you a clue to any potential problems with the machine.

• Verify the availability of replacement parts before you buy, and think about how much you need to invest before it is operational.

• Obtain from the owner whatever accessories, safety equipment, manuals, and documentation originally came with the tool. They will make the operation safer and repairs and maintenance easier.

quality tool and a piece of trash. Generally, look them over and ensure they are in good condition. Check for bent parts or cracked castings. Clean them off a bit to make sure all the pieces are present, otherwise it may be impossible to find replacement parts. You can ignore a little surface rust, but if anything looks especially rusty or pitted then it's worth bypassing. Consider the price. Could you buy a new one for around the same amount of money? The answer may be yes, but a new one may not be of the same quality. One person's jointer plane is another's *objet d'art*. It's perfectly fine to pick up an old tool for its curiosity or decorative value, but be aware of what you're buying.

When purchasing more substantial tools like a table saw or a drill press, investigate the tool's history. You may be buying a saw from a hobbyist woodworker who has been puttering around with it in the basement, or from a contractor who has bounced it on and off his truck six days a week. Ideally, you'd like to find lightly used and well-cared-for tools.

Safety first

It's a lot easier to cut things off than stick them back on. This is as true for fingers and toes as it is for wood and metal.

Working with tools involves a degree of risk. You can reduce the risk significantly by using common sense and always paying close attention to what you are doing. When you are working, consider several factors: your ability, the worked materials, your equipment, and your surroundings. To be safe, each of these things should be under your control. You need to know of the proper methods and have the ability and skill to perform them.

When you are drowsy, distracted, or maybe not 100 per cent focused, mistakes happen and at best you will have screwed up your project by rushing it, or at worst, you will seriously injure yourself.

Prepare and protect yourself physically. If you are using anything with motors or moving parts, do not wear loose or flowing clothes or jewelry. If you have long hair, tie it back. You don't want to get anything caught or tangled in any machine operating at thousands of rpm. Horrible, painful accidents happen quickly. Wear decent shoes to avoid slipping and protect your feet from falling or sharp objects. Use any safety gear appropriate to the tool in use. This may include gloves, eye protection, a dust mask, hearing protection. Safety gear is discussed in more detail within the Storage and protection section in the Tool Guide (see page 200).

Know how your tool works and how it should be be operated. Do not disable any safety guards or devices. Do not force a tool to do a job for which it is not intended. Read and follow the instruction manual. If you are learning to use a tool, practice on some scrap until you feel comfortable and familiar with how it behaves. When you are working, you should always be in control of the tool. Mistakes happen and sometimes a tool behaves unexpectedly. Learn from these mistakes and figure out why they occurred. If you are unsure, ask someone. Something may be wrong with the tool or your technique.

Maintain your tools by keeping them clean. Keep cutters and blades sharp. A sharp tool is safer than a dull one because the blade moves smoothly through the work. Forcing a dull blade through the work piece can lead to accidents.

Be aware of your actions and movements and think out the technique before you start a particular task. Where are you and your hands positioned in relation to the tool? Will these positions change as the work progresses? Where will the tool go if it should slip? Where will your hands go if they too should slip? Think ahead and always anticipate what could go wrong and adjust your setup to avoid any nasty consequences.

Safety considerations:

- Pesticide treatment applied to pressure-treated lumber contains arsenic and should never be used indoors nor should food be eaten in close proximity.

- Certain exotic woods can provoke an allergic reaction in some people.

- Paints, finishes, and solvents containing dangerous fumes should be worked only in well-ventilated areas and be stored away from potential sparks, flames, or other heat sources.

- Long-term exposure to sawdust has been shown to cause respiratory problems. Wear a dust mask or respirator to protect your lungs when sanding, cutting, or working with drywall and concrete.

- Dispose of waste and debris in a safe and environmentally sound manner. Read the product's label or ask the retailer if there are any special precautions to take for disposal.

- Spread out paint or solvent-soaked rags to dry in a well-ventilated area prior to disposal. Don't toss wadded-up rags into the trash can as the heat generated by the evaporation of any solvent can cause combustion.

- Do not burn pressure-treated lumber and aerosol cans.

- Cluttered work areas are hazardous, and you can also waste a lot of time looking for tools. Hastily run extension cords are particularly dangerous (see also page 207).

- Make sure other people—especially children—are safely out harm's way before you start working.

- Try to reduce or eliminate any distractions while you are working. If the phone rings or someone calls your name, finish what you are doing before you address it.

Finally, know the limits of your skills and knowledge. It's fun and exciting to try new things, but don't bite off more than you can chew. If possible, plan your projects to build on the experience of your previous one. Working this way builds up your repertoire of skills, but be honest with yourself when you decide to take on something new.

While you can't eliminate all the risk in using tools, you can intelligently manage it. In doing so, your projects will be safer, more enjoyable, and ultimately more successful and satisfying.

2 TOOL KITS

Apartment kit

Components

- **Phillips™ screwdrivers, at least one small and one medium-size (page 168)**
- **Slotted screwdriver, at least one small and one medium-size (page 168)**
- **Adjustable wrenches, one small, one medium-size (page 172)**
- **Pliers (page 176)**
- **Needle-nosed pliers with wire cutter (page 176)**
- **Claw hammer (page 153)**
- **Putty knife (page 197)**
- **Utility knife (page 66)**
- **Tape measure (page 50)**
- **Cordless drill (page 102)**
- **Drill bits (page 94)**
- **Torpedo level (page 60)**
- **File (page 130)**
- **Flashlight**
- **A small plastic box for hardware**
- **Can of penetrating lubricant**
- **Duct tape**
- **Toolbox (page 206)**

If your apartment is only marginally larger than an office cubicle, there are still going to be many occasions when you will require at least a few fundamental tools. Whether you want to put your personal touch on your surroundings by installing blinds or shades, or you simply want to make the place habitable by assembling flatpack furniture, this kit should get you started. All of this will fit in a medium-size toolbox and prepare you for most things you'll run across as an apartment dweller.

You may have every intention of talking a friend into helping you hang your pictures or put up some shelves, in which case, it's a lot easier to lure them in if you already have tools on hand. It's even better if you know which tool to hand to them. Assisting someone with more experience is often the best way to learn.

You may even graduate beyond using the screwdriver to open paint cans, to installing a washer or dryer, replacing door locks or repairing your bicycle. And when you are ready to move on you will have the tool to patch the small holes in the walls to get your deposit back.

Auto kit

Components

- **Phillips™ screwdrivers, small, medium, large (page 168)**
- **Slotted screwdrivers, small, medium, large (page 168)**
- **Adjustable wrench (page 172)**
- **Small set of wrenches (page 172)**
- **Locking pliers (page 179)**
- **Pliers with wire cutters (page 176)**
- **Torque wrench (page 175)**
- **Pocket knife**
- **Jumper cables**
- **Battery terminal brush**
- **Spare fuses**
- **1 quart of oil**
- **Duct tape**
- **Can of penetrating lubricant**
- **Flashlight**
- **Gloves**
- **Handiwipes and a rag**
- **Band-aids**
- **Toolbox (page 206)**
- **Flares or reflective triangles**
- **Blanket (for emergencies)**

Your idea of auto repair may be calling AAA on your cell phone, but it makes sense to have a set of tools in your vehicle. The older the vehicle, the more important it is to have a tool kit on hand. Generally, the cheaper the vehicle, the simpler it is to repair. (You need only five wrenches and a couple of screwdrivers to disassemble the majority of a Honda Civic.) Even if you don't plan doing any major mechanical work nor want to change the oil or the air filter, necessities like changing a tire, jump-starting a neighbor's flat battery, or minor chores like changing bulbs, replacing trim, etc., usually require at least a few basic tools. Some items in this kit overlap with the Apartment and Plumbing kit, but if you can purchase duplicates, keep your auto kit permanently in the trunk for running repairs on the roadside or emergencies.

Determine whether you need standard or metric tools. If you're unsure, check the vehicle manual or give the dealer a call. It may be handy to have a few of each system in your kit.

Home kit

Components

- **Workbench with vise (page 112)**
- **Toolbox(es) (page 206)**
- **6-foot ladder (page 208)**
- **Extension cord (page 207)**
- **Claw hammer (page 153)**
- **Combination handsaw (page 73)**
- **Hacksaw (page 79)**
- **Set Phillips™ screwdrivers (page 168)**
- **Set slotted screwdrivers (page 168)**
- **Set wrenches (page 172)**
- **Socket wrench set (page 174)**
- **Pliers (page 176)**
- **Electric drill (page 101)**
- **Twist drill bits (page 94)**
- **24-inch level (page 60)**
- **Combination square (page 57)**
- **Tape measure (page 50)**
- **Basic set butt chisels (page 126)**
- **Mill file (page 130)**
- **Rasp or Surform (page 130)**
- **Two 24-inch bar clamps (page 118)**
- **Two 4-inch C-clamps (page 120)**
- **Flashlight**

Once you make the big jump into home ownership, you will suddenly have more maintenance issues to deal with. If you are fortunate, the house has been well kept by the previous owners, and you may need only to continue periodic maintenance, or your house may be new. However, fixtures do deteriorate, your tastes may change, and at some point large-scale repair or renovation may be required. The tools you need then depend on how hands-on you intend to be as a home owner. Unless you have a handyman on call 24 hours a day, as king or queen of your castle, it will be up to you deal with maintenance and general repairs, and be prepared for emergencies.

If you are planning some carpentry, remodeling such as constructing a new porch or deck, or some serious renovation work, additional tools and a dedicated workspace may be necessary, but this kit combined with the Apartment kit, provides a collection of tools that address most of the major household and general home maintenance needs.

Plumbing kit

Components

- **Toilet plunger**
- **Drain auger (page 209)**
- **Flashlight**
- **Screwdrivers and wrenches (see Home tool kit, and pages 168 and 172)**
- **Offset screwdrivers (page 168)**
- **Water pump pliers (page 178)**
- **Locking pliers (page 179)**
- **Pipe wrenches (page 172)**
- **Tubing cutter (page 72)**
- **Teflon tape**
- **Electrical tape**
- **Emery cloth (page 191)**
- **Rubber gloves**

For soldering copper pipe you'll also need:

- **Gas torch (page 187)**
- **Spark lighter**
- **Solder and flux (page 186)**
- **Brass bristle brush**

Plumbing maintenance is always inconvenient, and usually very unpleasant. When you have a clogged drain line or burst water pipes you will want to have the right tool immediately to hand.

Fortunately, many simple problems can be solved without calling in professional help. Minor leaks and worn faucet problems can be repaired by replacing a few parts, which are readily available from hardware stores or plumbing suppliers. But catastrophic problems can occur: a pipe freezes and bursts apart, you drill into a wall and accidentally find a water line. Whether or not you intend handling minor repairs, you will still be there in the front line until the professionals arrive. It will be up you to shut the water off, and if possible, isolate the leak to minimize as much as possible damage to the surrounding area.

The key to undertaking any plumbing task is knowing where water tanks, shut-off valves, meters, and drains are located. Find and clearly label the main supply shut-off and other exposed plumbing lines before an emergency happens.

Electrical kit

Components

- **Combination wire stripper/crimper (page 71)**
- **Lineman's pliers (page 177)**
- **Needle-nosed pliers (page 176)**
- **Circuit tester (page 62)**
- **Insulated screwdrivers (page 168)**
- **Electrical tape**
- **Assortment of wire nuts**

For repairs to appliances or electronics you may also want:

- **Soldering gun (page 186)**

Running new wiring, adding or modifying an electrical panel, or adding new junction boxes are best left to the professionals. Some building jurisdictions may leave you with no choice, and it is always wise to be cautious of electricity. If in doubt, call a licensed electrician.

There are, however, many tasks you can perform safely, such as rewiring a lamp, installing a ceiling fan, or repairing an appliance. Before you start, research the project and safe working procedures, and ask someone experienced for help or advice. Understand each step before you proceed.

Never work on a live circuit. Shut the power off to the circuit at the breaker panel and be sure the device is off line before you work. Do not stand in or near water, on a metal ladder or stool or touch any pipes when you're doing electrical work. Avoid making yourself a conductor for electricity to ground through.

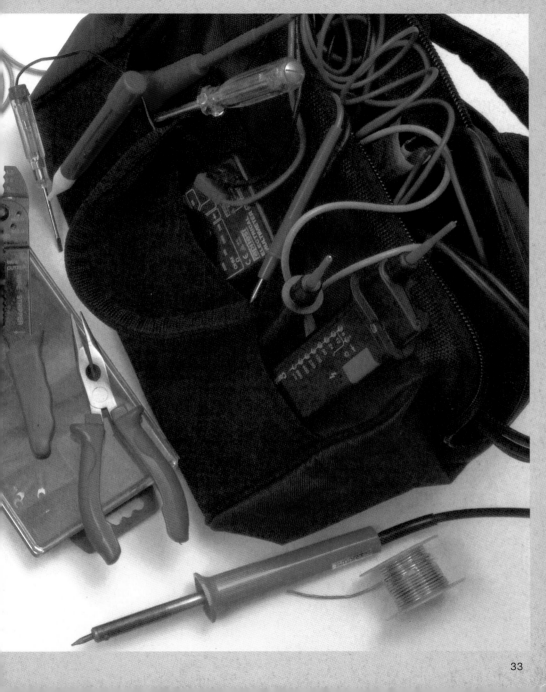

Machine and metal work kit

Components

- **Set Phillips™ screwdrivers (page 168)**
- **Set slotted screwdrivers (page 168)**
- **Set crescent/box wrenches (page 172)**
- **Socket wrench set (page 174)**
- **Can of penetrating lubricant**
- **Assortment of files (page 130)**
- **Aviation snips (page 69)**
- **Pliers (page 176)**
- **Hacksaw (page 79)**
- **Locking pliers (page 179)**
- **Vises (page 114)**
- **Bench grinder/wire wheel (page 145)**
- **Taps and dies (page 147)**
- **Emery cloth (page 191)**
- **Steel wool (page 192)**

It is a fact of modern life that we are surrounded by metal products and machinery, and many tasks around the home require the tightening, or removal of nut-bolt and screw-type connections. The Machine and metal work kit will help you accomplish that type of task. These tools allow you to cut and bend light-gauge sheet metal for ductwork, metal studs, or flashing, and metal siding. The grinder, files, and hacksaw allow you to cut, shape, and dress substantial pieces of metal. These techniques and tools will be what you look for when cutting bolts, threaded rod and metal bar stock to length, or more simply sharpening the garden tools and lawn mower blades.

A wire wheel attached to the bench grinder and a few grades of steel wool will quickly clean up rusted or pitted tools or parts.

Child's kit

Components

- **Small hammer (page 153)**
- **Small saw (page 73)**
- **Pliers (page 176)**
- **Two screwdrivers (page 168)**
- **Tape measure (page 50)**
- **Small box nails and screws (page 160)**
- **Sandpaper (page 191)**
- **Hand drill with bits (page 98)**
- **Pencil (page 52)**
- **Small toolbox (page 206)**

Working together on projects is a great way to spend time with your kids. Children learn a lot by working alongside you, by passing you the tools, or just holding the flashlight. Keep a box of scraps for them to paw through, and you may soon find yourself sharing your shop with a young and talented woodworker.

Build a small workbench alongside your own. Outfit it with a small clamp-on vise for easier nailing or sanding. If you don't have a dedicated workspace and the kids are working on the kitchen floor, consider keeping a small sheet of plywood around to lay down for them to work on. It will protect the floor from tools and stray nails.

Once they are familiar with how to use a few basic hand tools, you can encourage your children to create things of their own, but it is essential an adult is always present to supervise children when they are using tools, to demonstrate and ensure safe use.

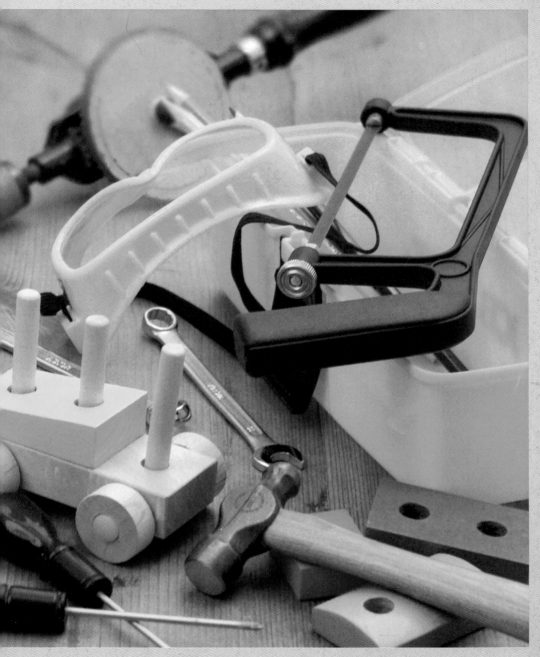

Craft kit

Components

- **Hobby knife set (page 67)**
- **Snap-off utility knife (page 66)**
- **Cutting mat**
- **Steel rule (page 48)**
- **Bench hook (page 116)**
- **Needle-nosed pliers (page 176)**
- **Round-nosed pliers (page 176)**
- **Set jewelers' screwdrivers (page 168)**
- **Hand drill and bits (page 98)**
- **Tweezers**
- **Clothespins (to use as clamps)**
- **Scissors**
- **Bone folder**
- **Needle files (page 130)**
- **Emery board, fine sandpaper (page 191)**
- **Adhesive (page 181)**
- **Small paintbrushes**
- **Desk lamp**

There are as many tools designed specifically for crafts as there are for standard use. Whether it is measuring, cutting, shaping, joining, the tools in a Craft kit allow you to work with different materials, even small scale. The tools suitable for creative tasks will often work for regular repairs and maintenance of small items around the house.

To create your own artwork and printed matter, such as unique greeting cards, brochures, and invitations, a good knife, rule, and bone folder help provide your work with a professional finish.

Small-scale work does not require a dedicated space. A lot of projects can be done at the kitchen table. If you don't have a spot where you can leave your materials sitting out, it's best to have a small toolbox for the tools, and use plastic boxes to keep the parts of your project together while it is in progress.

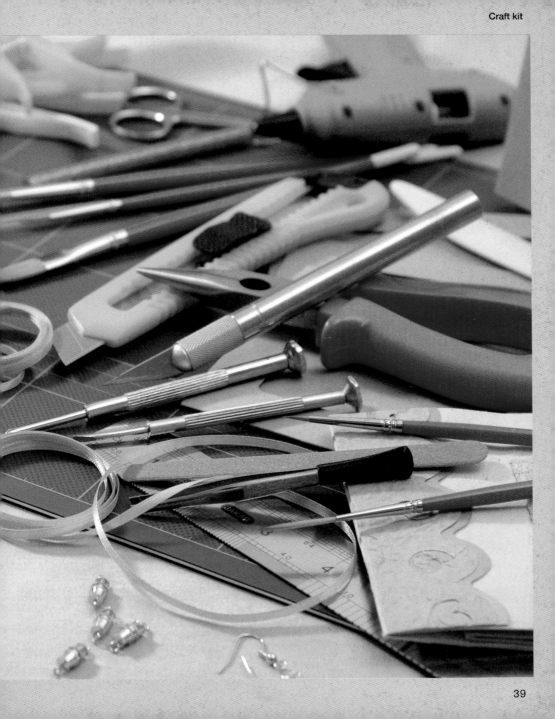

A home workshop

A workshop is a safe, efficient, dedicated area in which you can work comfortably, whether it is a full-scale woodworking shop in an outbuilding, or the corner of the sitting room where you want to build model airplanes. Whatever your situation, there is a recipe for the ideal shop, or functioning work space.

Space and layout
- Work surfaces. A good, solid, clear work surface is the heart of a workshop.

- Tool storage. Accessible, organized storage of your tools is essential when they are not in use, to extend their life and make your work more efficient.

- Material storage. Space for storage of raw materials, including scraps and leftovers. Hardware, finishes, and other supplies also need a home.

- Space to use equipment. Consider the space needed to maneuver material on and through machinery. Table saws are often in the center of a small shop ready to cut the largest pieces. If you want to run an 8-foot long board through the saw, then the saw should be at least 8 feet away from the wall in front and behind, otherwise you cannot run the board all the way through. Also account for safety zones around a machine.

- Assembly space. You will want to assemble your project without hindrance when using the other areas of the shop. If you plan to routinely work on large projects, you will need larger space. In a kitchen, food comes from refrigerator to the counter to the stove. In a workshop, material goes from storage to rough-milled, to finer work, and ultimately to finishing. Try to keep the sequence of work in mind when arranging your space.

- Access. Can you get raw materials into the space and finished projects out? (When Henry Ford built his first car, he had to knock out a wall of his shop before he could take it outside for a test drive. Effective, but not recommended.) If things are tight, consider rough cutting materials to size to bring them inside. Fabricate large projects in sections.

Utilities
- Power. Verify that you have sufficient circuits and outlets. Tools such as large table saws or planers require power of sufficient voltage and correct phase.

- Lighting. Good illumination is essential. Fluorescent fixtures are a cost-effective option. (Use clear plastic safety tubes over the bulbs.) Supplement ambient lighting with individual task lamps at the workbench. Paint the walls, floors, and ceilings in light colors to brighten spaces. If colors are important in your work, choose your lighting carefully, as color under incandescent light differs under daylight or fluorescent, and vice versa. Fluorescent bulbs are available with color rendering characteristics similar to daylight.

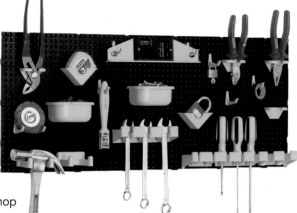

- Heating. Work in a warm, dry space. Humidity promotes rust on tools and fluctuations in the moisture level can cause wood to swell and shrink. If you have a base-ment shop, consider using a dehumidifier in the summer. Check regulations with your local Building Department and Fire Department before instaling heating devices in a shop space.

- Air quality. Make sure the space is properly ventilated, especially when using solvents or finishes. If you do a lot of sanding or sawing, consider an air filter or dust collection system. Otherwise, use a respirator or dust mask. Consider partitioning off an area to help confine the dust in the workshop.

Creating your own workshop

Few of us are blessed with an unlimited amount of space, and many of the above points willnaturally have to be reconciled with reality. Most hobbyists' workshops are in basements and garages, which have other uses like household storage, car parking, or laundry.

Start by drawing a top-scale floor plan of the space you do have. Then make paper cutouts (to the same scale as the plan) of the benches, shelves, and equipment that you plan to include in the shop. Try to project ahead a few years and anticipate what tools and equipment you may want to acquire and house in the future. Slide the cutouts around and play with them until you come up with your best solution. There are many excellent books available offering design guidance and tips and solutions.

You may need to compromise, but everything doesn't have to be absolutely perfect. Keep in mind your workshop will always be a work-in-progress. Priorities will change and evolve, and as your experience expands you will tailor the space to the way you work.

Once you've got a plan of action, go for it! Be safe and have fun!

Key to tool guide

To make looking for particular information easier to find, the following heads appear at the start of each entry.

• **Materials** that the tool is suitable for, such as wood, metal, plastic, glass, ceramic, etc.

• Which of the tool **kits** it appears in (if any) (see Tool Kits pages 22 to 39)

• **Price** range

$	0–25
$$	25–75
$$$	75–150
$$$$	150+

• Level of **necessity**

OOOOO	Absolute must-have
OOOO	Always useful
OOO	Specialized, but essential to certain tasks
OO	A luxury— it will make a task faster, more accurate or more enjoyable
O	Used once in a blue moon, so borrow or rent it when there's a blue moon

• Degree of **skill required** for its use

O	Anyone can use it
OO	There's a knack to it, but most folks can handle it
OOO	Experience with the tool, material and type of work are necessary

3 TOOL GUIDE

Measuring and layout

Measuring is involved in most phases of all but the simplest projects, and in each instance forms the basis for the work that follows, whether it is figuring out the shape, size, and location of a project, or determining the type and amount of materials required.

Layout markings guide the cut and shape of the work piece. Throughout a job, it is measuring that is required to verify size, square, level, or plumb. Time spent on measuring, preparing, and laying out pays dividends in the execution and in the final appearance of the job.

General rules

- "Measure twice, cut once" is top of the list. You want to be darn sure that the mark you've made is in the right spot, so measure, and then measure again.

- Precision is relative. Measurements and cuts to the nearest ⅛ inch are good enough when framing a garden shed,

Beginner's class

The finer points of using particular measuring devices are covered in the individual tool entries, but here are some initial basic terms, techniques, and tips to get you on your way.

1 When measuring large areas or buildings, it's helpful to draw a plan on which to note the dimensions.

2 Often when measuring, it's helpful to record or call out to your helper whether something is an *inside dimension* (ID) or an *outside dimension* (OD) in addition to the amount. It will help ensure that things will fit

properly down the road. ID and OD are often noted when dealing with pipe and tubing, because in some applications the inside dimension is critical, sometimes it is the outside that is. It's important to know which is the case for your project when buying material.

3 In most projects, cutting and joining pieces at 90° angles is a standard and key requirement. To do so, a try square or combination square is usually used to draw cutting lines and to verify built pieces.

4 To draw a line perpendicular to an edge, such as when marking where to cross cut a board, lay the blade flat on the face of the board and slide the other, thicker leg (called the stock) up against

when being too finicky is a waste of time. However, if you are making a jewelry box, much finer measures are more crucial and worth taking time over.

- Use a sharp pencil or a knife for accurate markings.

- When buying materials, buy extra to account for waste and faults. When buying wood, the ends may be split or have a few knots. Some extra length will allows for working around defects when cutting, or discarding any sections.

- Make a list of the pieces that are needed for a project to figure out how much material is needed. Draw out the boards or sheets of materials and how they will be cut. Try to use the material economically to minimize scraps.

- Pick one edge of the material to be the "working edge" on which measurements will be made and lines drawn square. This should be an edge that has been planed flat and square.

- Sometimes, you may ignore dimensions and go with what looks right. If you're hanging a long curtain rod in an old house that has settled over time, it may look better to hang the rod parallel to the sloping ceiling than to hang it truly level.

---

the edge. Since the stock is thicker than the blade, it hooks over the edge of the board, giving a good, firm alignment. For greatest accuracy, put the tip of your marking instrument down on the wood first, then slide the blade of the square up to it, rather than the other way around.

5 To check to see if the corner of a work piece is truly 90°, hold one leg of the square up to one side of the corner. Then slide it until the other leg of the square touches the opposite face of the corner. Both legs

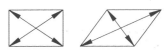

should sit tightly against the work piece. If they don't, you will see light through any gaps between the two, which means the corner is not square. Even the finest discrepancies become obvious this way.

6 If you don't have a square to hand, applying some basic geometry along with a tape measure or ruler will work instead. If an item has four square corners, then the measurement of the diagonals between them will each be equal. If the sides of the item are out of whack, then the diagonals will be unequal. This works just the same way whether checking the squareness of small items, such as frames or drawers, or on larger jobs, such as posts for a deck or laying out the badminton court in your backyard.

Steel rule

Materials:	**Wood**
	Metal
	Plastic
	Glass
	Ceramic
Kits:	**Home**
	Craft
Price:	**$**
Necessity:	**⬡⬡⬡⬡**
Skill level:	**⬡**

A *steel rule* is the simplest and most accurate measuring tool for use on precise layout work. Steel rulers are marked up in graduations of at least 1⁄16 inch. Some machinist's rules are marked in increments as fine as 1⁄100 inch. They are available in lengths of 6, 12, 18, and 24 inches. A 12- or 18-inch rule is adequate for general use.

To measure, look straight on to the measure point. If you look at it from the side, you will correct for perspective, which leads to inaccuracy. If zero is at the end of the rule, butt the rule and the object to be measured against a scrap block of wood. This will ensure the edges of both are aligned and make it easier to obtain an accurate measurement.

Line the rule along the edge of the item to be measured. If the end isn't square, leave the piece a little long to square it up later. Otherwise there is the risk of ending up with a short piece.

Steel rules also serve as a straightedge when cutting with a craft, hobby, or utility knife. To cut the straight edge, hold the knife perpendicular to the cutting surface to keep the blade from running under the straightedge. Keep your fingers back from the edge.

A rule with a cork backing will help prevent it from slipping while you cut. Look for etched numbers and graduations as they are durable and more accurate. Do not buy an aluminum rule if you need to do precise work or if you intend to use it as a straightedge. The numbers and marks are usually printed and a knife can cut into the soft aluminum.

TOP TOOL TIP
Clean up a tarnished steel rule with some fine steel wool and a light coat of wax.

Folding rule

Materials: **Wood**
Metal
Plastic
Glass
Ceramic
Price: **$$**
Necessity: **OOOO**
Skill level: **O**

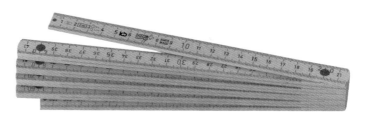

A *folding rule*, also called *zig zag* rule, is for measuring large objects, yet it folds for easy transport and storage. It was an early development in tools—indeed, a bronze folding rule was excavated from the ruins of Pompeii.

Folding rules commonly available today were first introduced in 1903. They are usually 6 or 8 feet long with several of the segments connected to each other by pivot joints. A sliding bar with graduations is often built into the first segment.

Measurement styles differ: feet and inches are used by carpenters; feet and tenths of feet are used by surveyors, and mason's rules are marked in brick courses. Most rules are made from boxwood and brass, though some are metal.

Folding rules have been largely eclipsed by tape measures, but they are straight and rigid when extended so they don't flop around, which is helpful when you are working alone. This is also helpful when measuring inside dimensions.

To do so, unfold as many segments as will fit inside the object you are measuring. Slide the brass bar out of the first segment to make up the difference. Then add the dimension on the brass bar to the length of the wood section you unfolded. Use this same method to check the measurements of a drawer or case for squareness.

When buying a zig zag rule, new or used, it is important to make sure the joints are snug. Keep the joints in good shape by cleaning and oiling them occasionally. Avoid putting too much sideways pressure on the connections, which can loosen them and make the rule less rigid and therefore less accurate.

Antique caliper rules

Small folding rules 12 to 24 inches long were once a standard tool of the trade, and well-kept antique rules are popular among tool collectors. A *caliper rule* has a hooked bar which slides out to measure the outside diameter of small objects.

Tape measure

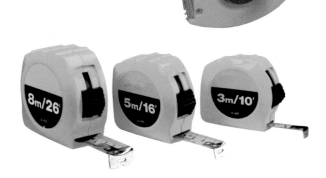

Materials: **Wood**
               Metal
               Plastic
               Glass
               Ceramic
Kits: **Apartment**
               Home
               Child's
Price: **$**
Necessity: **○○○○○**
Skill level: **⬡**

Even if you are measuring for curtains or checking if a chair will fit through the door on delivery, *tape measures* are essential.

Contemporary steel tape measures consist of a long steel tape arced in cross section. A hook is riveted to one end. The other end is hooked to a coiled spring housed in a plastic case. The spring will automatically retract the tape into the case when released. On some measures, a sliding button is provided to lock the tape in its extended position.

When purchasing a tape measure, first decide on a length. A 24-inch model is satisfactory for the household. Twelve feet is better when furniture shopping or apartment hunting.

Look for a durable tape that will extend to its length without being supported, known as "standout." The more standout, the easier it is to take measurements. Look too for a good case and lock mechanism.

To get a precise measurement, line up the 1-inch mark, rather than the end of the tape, at the start point, read the dimension, then subtract the extra inch.

To measure an outside dimension, hook the tape over the end of an object and pull the case down the length, laying it directly on the edge of the object. To measure an inside dimension, put the tape case in the corner of the "box" and pull the tape out to the opposite side. Read the measurement and add on the length of the case, which is often printed on its side. When taking an outside dimension, zero point is on the inside face of the hook. The reverse is true for measuring an inside dimension.

Variations:
Fabric tape measures are narrow 6-foot long tapes used to measure fabric.
Extra long tape measures are available in 80 feet, 100 feet, or longer and are for surveying, measuring large spaces, buildings, and property. They do not have a spring, but instead have a folding crank on the case to rewind the tape.

Calipers and dividers

Materials: **Wood**
Metal
Plastic
Glass
Ceramic
Price: **$$**
Necessity: **OOOO**
Skill level: **O**

1

2

Calipers, dividers, and compasses are used to transfer dimensions from one object to another.

Dividers have two straight legs with pointed ends. By setting the distance between the legs equal to the measured length, that measure is transferred as the dividers "walk" down a line to "step off" a series of identical measures (see figure 1).

A compass is a pair of dividers with a marking instrument on one leg. It will mark the perfect circle by being swung 360° on its point, and will "scribe" an object to match the profile of something it abutts, as when making a counter or cabinet fit tightly against a wall. The compass is used to draw a line parallel to the surface of the wall (see figure 2). The counter is cut back to the line and set in place. The compass must be set perpendicular to the surface being copied. The same method is used to trim the base of a cabinet to sit level on an uneven floor or to cut a notch out of a material to fit around a piece of molding.

The instrument works well on a flat plane, but is limited with 3-D objects; for example, the tips of the dividers cannot touch opposite sides of a ball. This is why calipers evolved. The legs of outside calipers flare out and then back inward to reach around an object. To turn four matching legs for a stool on a lathe, use calipers to mark the dimensions of the first one and ensure a match for the other three.

Inside calipers work in a similar way, except their legs turn outward at the bottom to measure an inside dimension.

Shop for instruments with fine tips and an adjustment system and which pivot with little play to hold material securely in place.

Variations:
Drafting compasses and dividers are precision instruments used for fine work or drawing. Reasonably priced sets are available at art and office supply stores.

Pencils

Materials: Wood
Metal
Plastic
Glass
Ceramic
Kits: Apartment
Home
Machine and metal work
Craft
Price: $
Necessity: OOOOO
Skill level: O

A *carpenter's pencil* is fat and ideal for rough work. They are flat so they don't roll and their thick body and the lead make them durable. Pocket-sized sharpeners are specifically designed to accept the broad carpenter's pencil. Because the lead is so big and the marks are thick, they are not well suited for much beyond rough cutting material to size.

No.2 pencil. These pick up where the carpenter's pencil leaves off. They are cheap and can be easily sharpened, but they are not ideal for precision work unless you are fastidious about maintaining a fine point. Twirling the pencil in your fingers as you draw a line allows the tip to wear as evenly as possible.

A *drafting lead holder* is an alternative to a wood pencil. It has a plastic barrel with spring-loaded jaws holding individual leads. A special sharpener is used with these to maintain a very fine point. The twirling trick works well with these too.

Mechanical pencil. A 0.5 mm drafting pencil is the best device, short of a marking knife, for performing fine layout work. Because the lead is very thin, you always get a consistent line thickness.

TOP TOOL TIPS
- When drawing a line, put the pencil on the mark first and slide the straightedge or square up to it. This ensures your line begins in exactly the right spot.
- Use a vinyl drafting eraser because it smudges less than other erasers.
- Keep a few white pencils around. They show up better on dark materials than regular graphite pencils.

Marking gauge

Materials: Wood
Price: $$
Necessity: OOO
Skill level: O

1

A *marking gauge* is a simple device used to scribe a line parallel to an edge. It is used to mark out lines to make cuts for wood joinery. There is a wood bar, or beam, about 8 inches long passing through a square hole in a block of wood called the *stock*. The stock slides up and down the beam and has a thumbscrew threaded into it to hold it in place. Often these two pieces have brass strips inlaid in them to protect the wear surfaces. A sharpened steel scribe is on the end of the beam.

To use the gauge, hold the stock against the edge of the board and slide the beam through until the scribe is located the required distance from the edge. Tighten the thumbscrew to lock everything in place (*see figure 1*). (To adjust, tap the end of the beam in the bench top.) Hold the gauge firmly against the edge of the board and, with steady pressure on the scribe, push or pull the gauge along the board's length. This will scratch a line in the face of the board parallel to the edge the stock was riding on. Tip the gauge a bit in the direction of travel and the gauge will move more evenly.

A combination square can be used as a substitute marking gauge (see page 57).

Variations:
Mortising gauge. There are two scribes, not one, on the end of the beam. One is fixed in place and the other is attached to a sliding brass bar which can be moved by turning an adjustment screw. The gauge is used to scribe two parallel lines defining the two sides of a mortise. Some mortising gauges have a third scribe in the opposite face of the beam so you have the option of scribing one line or two.

Cutting gauge has a small, round-tipped blade held in place with a small wedge. It is used to make marks across the grain. Replacing the curved blade with a pointed one allows the gauge to cut strips of thin materials, such as wood veneer.

Scratch awl and marking knife

Materials: **Wood**
Price: **$$**
Necessity: **OOO**
Skill level: **O**

These two items are used to mark out guidelines for wood joinery by scoring a very thin line on the surface of the wood. This is an accurate method, but it does leave scratches on the wood.

The *scratch awl* is used to mark a centerpoint of a hole. A little divot is left in the wood by the point of the awl, providing a spot for a drill tip to rest, and making the starting of each hole easier and more accurate. It looks like an ice pick, but with a shorter, stiffer shaft. A broad, oval handle nestles into the palm of your hand to allow you to use the force of your forearm to press the tip into material.

Twist drill bits have a wider tip than brad point bits so they need a bigger divot to settle in (see more on bits on page 94). Rock the awl around to enlarge the mark. When using the awl for scribing lines, ensure the tip is sharp or it will make too broad a mark.

A *marking knife* is a better choice for making lines across the grain because it cleanly severs the grain on the face of the wood. Japanese knives consist of a small bar of soft steel with a section of high-carbon steel forged onto one end. This is ground to form a cutting edge. Western knives typically have a short steel blade mounted in a wood handle. Blades of marking knives are beveled on the left side, the right, or both sides. A non-beveled side is intended to ride along the straightedge, so whichever style you choose depends on whether you are left- or right-handed.

Chalk line

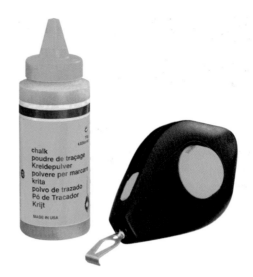

Materials: **Wood**
Metal
Plastic
Glass
Ceramic
Price: **$$**
Necessity: **OOO**
Skill level: **O**

A *chalk line* is 50 to 100 feet of string wound inside a case containing colored chalk. When in use, the string is pulled out and unwound over a surface, stretched taut, plucked, and released. The string snaps back against the surface, depositing a line of chalk dust, known as "snapping a line." A small folding crank mounted on the side of the case rewinds the line.

This is useful for marking cut lines when rough cutting a sheet of plywood to size, but more often it is used for large-scale layout work, such as hanging wallpaper, positioning shelves and cabinets, or instaling a countertop.

Prior to chalk lines, a string was pulled over a charred piece of wood called a smut stick. Snapping the line would leave a trail of soot behind. In Japan, a fine silk string was wrapped around a small wheel and pulled out through a tray containing cotton wadding soaked with ink.

Contemporary chalk lines have a teardrop-shaped metal or plastic case.

Look for a durable case. Most have some type of mechanism to lock the line in place, making it easier to pull the line tight to snap it, and enabling you to use it as a plumb bob (see page 59).

Try square

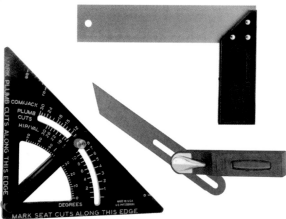

Materials: **Wood**
Metal
Plastic
Glass
Ceramic
Kits: **Home**
Price: **$$**
Necessity: ⬦⬦⬦⬦⬦
Skill level: ⬦

Many construction processes depend on right angles, so it is important to have a tool which provides a reliable measurement of a 90° angle.

The *try square* is made of a thin, 8- or 12-inch long flat steel "blade" and a short, thick hardwood "stock." The two are riveted together to form a precise L shape, and right-angle, both inside and outside. The inside face of the stock is faced with brass to maintain accuracy.

To check if an outside corner is square, hold the inside of the stock up to one face of the corner and slide it until the blade touches the other face. The face must touch along its entire length. Do the same to check whether the board is square.

To draw a line perpendicular to an edge, lay the blade flat on the face of the board and slide the stock up against the edge. Because the stock is thicker than the blade, it hooks over the edge, giving firm alignment. For greatest accuracy, put the tip of your marker on the wood first, then slide the square up to it, rather than the other way around.

Variations:
An *Engineer's square* is smaller and more accurate than the try square. The blade and the stock are steel. There is a notch cut in the stock where it meets the blade to prevent the square from rocking if there is a burr on the edge of a corner. Commonly available in sizes from 3 to 8 inches, they are excellent for layout work and setting up or calibrating tools and equipment.
A *speed square* is for rough work, such as framing lumber. It is a single triangular piece of aluminum, with a lip on one leg to hook over the edge of a board. Its casting is thick enough to serve as a cutting edge to run the bottom plate of a circular saw along when crosscutting boards.
A *sliding T-bevel's* blade is not fixed at 90°, and is free to slide and pivot until tightened in place. The T-bevel can duplicate an odd angle of an existing condition.

Combination square

Materials: **Wood**
Metal
Plastic
Glass
Ceramic
Kits: **Home**
Price: **$**
Necessity: ⬡⬡⬡⬡⬡
Skill level: ⬡

1

The *combination square* is used much like a try square, but has additional functions. It consists of a blade and a stock. The stock slides along the length of the blade or can be removed completely. The blade is usually 12 inches long and 1 inch wide with a half-round groove running down the center of one side. The blade slides through a slot in the stock and inside the slot is a key to engage the groove in the blade. When the thumbscrew attached to this key is tightened, the blade and stock are locked together. Loosening the screw allows the stock to slide up and down.

The stock is cast as a single piece of steel and has one side facing 90° to the blade and the other at 45° to the blade. A bubble level vial is built into it and a little sleeve holds a short scribe.

The try square is a more accurate tool, but for general work, the combination square stock is smaller, it has less bearing area on the edge, and the shape allows the marking or checking of 45° angles as well.

The square can also be used to measure the depth of a hole or mortise. Clean out the bottom of the hole, insert the end of the blade, and slide the stock down until it rests on the rim of the hole. Tighten the thumbscrew, then pull the rule out and read the dimension (*see figure 1*).

The combination square can be used as a marking gauge. Set the stock at the desired dimension, place the blade on the surface to be marked, and align the stock along the edge. Hold the square in place with one hand and a pencil at the end of the blade with your other. Often there is a notch at the end of the blade for this purpose. Slowly pull the square and the pencil down the board at the same time, drawing your line.

A drywall T-square is used as a cutting edge, and assists in making straight cuts in sheets of drywall. They are usually 48 inches long and can reach across a 4- x 8-foot sheet of drywall. You can disassemble it for easy transport.

Framing square

Materials: **Wood**
Metal
Plastic
Glass
Ceramic
Kits: **Craft**
Price: **$**
Necessity: **OOOO**
Skill level: **O**

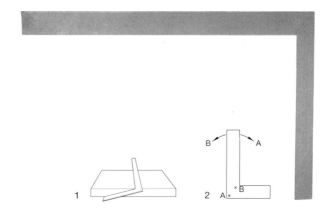

Contemporary *framing squares* consist of an L-shaped piece of steel or aluminum. One leg, called the blade, is 24 inches long; the other, called the tongue, is 16 inches. The corner where the two meet is called the heel.

Until the early 1800s most framing squares were made of wood, with wooden pegged joints in the heel. Vermont black-smith named Silas Hawes changed all that in 1817. Tired of using the delicate wood squares of the day, he hammer-welded two saw blades together, aligned them, and inscribed it with inch marks. He patented the instrument and made a tidy profit.

Use a framing square to verify measurements for inside and outside corners as for a try square (see page 56). For best results, let one leg of the square drop over the edge of the board and hold it tight to the face. The other leg of the square will not lie flat on the board, but you can draw a line along the edge of the square (*see figure 1*).

Some framing squares have reference tables inscribed on the face of the legs to assist in calculating rafter heights, lengths of diagonal corner braces, the number of board feet in a piece of lumber, or other construction calculations.

Treat a square with care tol maintain its accuracy. You can verify its squareness in the same way as the try square. Adjust by tapping the inside or outside corner of the heel (at points A to B, *see figure 2*), with a hammer and a center punch, to open or close the angle of the square

Plumb bob

Materials:	**Wood**
	Metal
	Plastic
	Glass
	Ceramic
Kits:	**Home**
Price:	**$–$$**
Necessity:	**OOOO**
Skill level:	**O**

A *plumb bob* is simply a pointed weight on a string. When the end of the string is tied to a high point, the weight hangs freely, to provide a true vertical or plumb line. This is useful for two reasons. It allows an item adjacent to the plumb line to be compared to determine if the object is plumb. And it also allows the accurate alignment of a point on the ground with a point above it.

This process is used to locate surveying equipment over a specified benchmark. For more everyday work, the plumb bob will enable you to ensure a hole in the ceiling is directly above a point or hole in the floor. This is helpful when installing pipes or ductwork, or mounting a fan or ceiling light fixture in the center of a room.

Plumb bobs vary in price and design. The inexpensive makes are hexagonal lumps of steel with a point on one end. More lavish models are made in burnished brass with removable or replaceable steel tips. The steel tip stores safely within the body of the bob when not in use.

Level

Materials: **Wood**
Metal
Plastic
Glass
Ceramic
Kits: **Apartment**
Home
Price: **$$**
Necessity: **OOOO**
Skill level: **O**

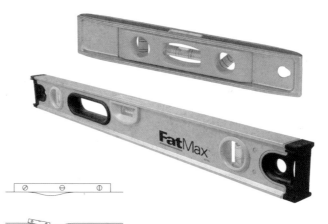

1

A *level* is used to determine if something is, indeed, level. The instrument incorporates small transparent vials, usually made of plastic, containing a bubble trapped in colored alcohol or oil. The tool is calibrated so that when it is level, the bubble rests between the marks. Most contemporary levels contain three vials—one to check level, one to check plumb, and one to verify a 45° angle. Each bubble reaffirms the reading of the other two.

Levels range in length from 8 inches up to 6 feet. A long level gives best results when the frame needs to bridge surface imperfections (*see figure 1*). A 12-inch level fits neatly into a toolbox, although a 24-inch level is more convenient when hanging shelves or wall cabinets.

Levels come in different styles. Small ones (8 to 12 inches), called *torpedo levels*, have a solid body and taper toward the ends. Levels of 24 inches or longer are available in three forms—extruded I-beam, wood, and extruded box beams. The

extruded I-beam levels are usually aluminum, I-shaped in section, and the least expensive. Masons prefer levels made of wood with an I-beam core because mortar and concrete does not stick to the wood surface. Extruded box beams are rectangular in cross section and are the stiffest of the lot.

Before purchasing a level, test it for accuracy. Place the level on a flat surface and note where the bubble falls. Keep the same edge on the counter, rotate the level 180°. The bubble should remain in the same place. Place the opposite edge on the counter and repeat the process. To check for plumb: place the level against a vertical surface, note the position of the bubble, keep the same end up, flip it to the alternative face to touch the wall. The bubble should be in the same spot in both configurations.

Some models will allow you to fine-tune the position of the vial to correct the calibration.

Water level

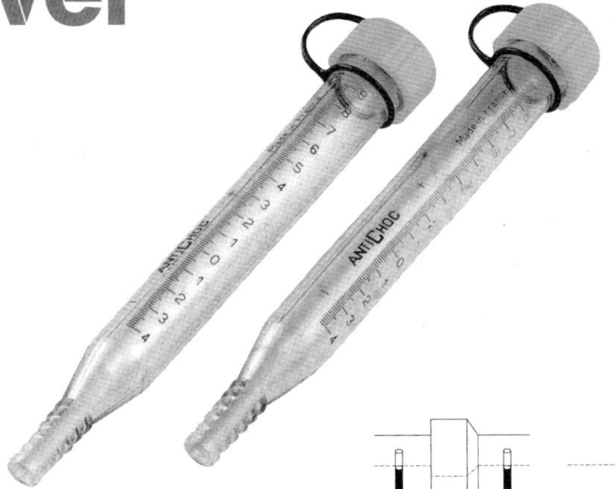

Materials: **Wood**
Metal
Plastic
Glass
Ceramic
Price: **$**
Necessity: **OOO**
Skill level: **O**

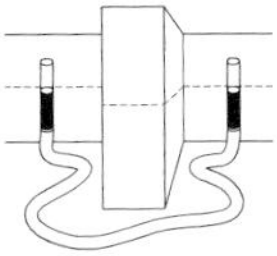

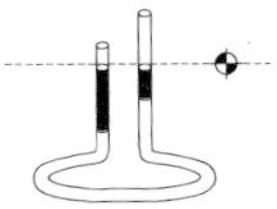

Water seeks its own level. If you need to ensure a particular elevation across a room, across a yard, or on opposite sides of an obstruction, a *water level* is the cheapest, easiest tool to use.

A water level kit consists of a pair of clear tubes that thread onto each end of a garden hose or a length of flexible tubing. A snap-on cap at the end of each tube allows you to lay the garden hose down without water leaking out. Alternatively, you can improvise using some clear tubing and duct tape.

To operate the water level, fill the hose with enough water so that each clear tube is half full. The water will then level itself (*see figure 1*). Note the surface of the water in the two tubes is at the same elevation, though it may not fall in the same place on the tube (*see figure 2*).

Circuit and continuity testers

Materials:	**Wiring**
	Electricity
Kits:	**Electrical**
Price:	**$–$$**
Necessity:	**○○○**
Skill level:	**○○**

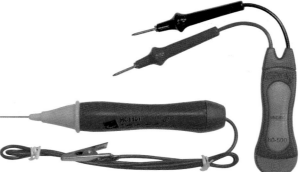

An electrical circuit is the path that electricity takes through a length of wiring, through connections, or components as it travels from point A to point B. Each of these tools is used to perform a particular test on a circuit.

A *circuit tester* is used on household socket points to determine whether they are "live" and have electricity flowing through them. This is a good way to check that power has indeed been cut to a point prior to working on it. They can also be used to determine whether a power point is properly grounded. The tester has a small plastic body with a light built into it. Two insulated leads run from the body and end with two bare metal probes. While holding the leads' insulated handles, these probes are inserted in the slots of the socket outlet. If the light comes on, the circuit is live. Some testers have multiple lights that are designed to turn on at a particular voltage, allowing you to confirm the voltage of the circuit.

A *continuity tester* is used to check for faults or shorts in a component. The tester has a battery built into its handle to provide a power source. On one end of the handle is a bare metal probe, on the other is an insulated lead with a clip at the end. The clip and the probe are connected internally so that when you touch them to one another, or touch each to the opposite ends of a wire, a circuit is completed and a light inside the handle comes on. There must be a continuous, unbroken path (a circuit) between the probe and the clip for the light to turn on. If you apply the clip and the probe to two parts of a component and the light fails to come on, this confirms the path is incomplete and that you have a short circuit. By applying the tester to different spots on the path, you can home in on the location of the failure.

Multimeter

Materials: **Electrical components**
Kits: **Electrical**
Price: **$$**
Necessity: **OOO**
Skill level: **OO**

The *multimeter* is more sophisticated than the testers shown on page 62. It can be used to diagnose and track down faults in home and in automotive electronics, appliances, motors, switches, and outlets. While the tool is simple to use, knowledge of electricity and wiring is necessary to understand the results.

The meter is a handheld device with an analog or digital display and a switch that determines the reading to be taken. A pair of insulated lead wires with metal probes plug into the body of the meter. The probes are touched to different parts of a circuit in the item being tested and the reading is shown on the display.

The multimeter has an internal power source, so it can be used to test for continuity (see page 62). It will also read voltage (measured in volts), which is how much electricity is available to a circuit. It can measure the amount of electrical current (amps) that is flowing through the circuit and can also determine the amount

of resistance (ohms) present within it. Each is related to the others: i.e, current = voltage / resistance.

The best way to understand this is to think of water in a pipe. Voltage is just like water pressure. Current is like the flow rate through the pipe, and resistance is like an obstruction to flow within the pipe. On an item of electrical equipment, the current and resistance need to operate within a certain range for a device to function correctly. The multimeter verifies that components are working and tracks down any that are not. It can do so for a range of current and voltage levels, from watch batteries to household current.

Current and voltage measurements are taken when electricity is flowing through the circuit. There is a danger of electric shock if performed improperly and only experienced users should carry out tests. If you are interested in electronics or electrical devices, the multimeter's versatility is indispensable.

Cutting

At least one of the stages in most projects involves cutting a material to size. The most important factors to take into consideration when selecting which cutting tool to use will be the type of material and whether the cut is straight or curved. Other things to consider are how coarse or precise the cut needs to be, and how to do it in the safest possible manner.

The keys on each cutting tool entry are to indicate which tools are appropriate for a particular material and the descriptions of the tools discuss the qualities of the cut you can expect from each.

There are other general points to keep in mind when choosing a tool, laying out the material, and setting up for a cut.

General rules
• A rip cut is the term given to a cut in a piece of wood that runs parallel to the grain. A cross cut is a cut that runs across the grain. There are saws tailored to each type of cut and others that are designed to do both.

• Always use the right cutting tool for the job. In general, the smaller the teeth on a saw, the finer the cut and the smoother

Beginner's class

While less tiring methods are available, using a hand saw is still the simplest, cheapest, and in some cases the quickest way to cut a piece of wood to size. It's fairly simple, but like any skill, a bit of practice helps.

1 The first step is to use a ruler or square to mark the location of the cut with a straight line. Then place the item to be cut on a pair of sawhorses or clamp it in a vise or to a tabletop. The goal is to make sure the work piece is adequately supported

and unable to move around as the cut is made. Once this is done, you're ready to start sawing.

2 Hold the saw in one hand, with your index finger pointing down the handle.

3 To start a cut, place the blade on the waste side of the cut line and hold your thumb against the side to steady it.

the finish. The larger the teeth, the faster the cut and the rougher the finish (see more on this on page 73).

• A saw's kerf is the gap left in the wood after the blade passes through, which in the case of table saws and circular saws can be as much as ⅛ inch. When making multiple parallel cuts the amount of material lost to kerfs can quickly add up and this needs to be taken into account when measuring.

• Examine the material to be cut for knots, nails, defect or blemishes that may affect the cut, the appearance, or strength of the finished piece. If possible, adjust the layout to avoid them.

• Act out the cut beforehand, especially if it is to be long. Ensure the work will be adequately supported throughout and is not off balance or in an awkward position as the blade moves through the material.

• Do a test cut on some scrap material first, especially if you have recently adjusted the tool, or it is new to you.

• Line up the blade on the waste side of the cut mark, otherwise there is the risk of the piece being cut too short by an amount equal to the width of the kerf. Draw an X on the waste side of the cut to identify it.

• Make sure nothing is in the path of the blade. This includes power cords and fingers or other extremities. When you are cutting larger pieces of material that are supported on a table or sawhorses, look underneath the work piece to make sure nothing will be hit by the blade.

4 Arrange yourself so that your hand, elbow and shoulder are in line with the saw blade and the cut line. At a shallow angle, pull the blade back a few times to establish a cutting slot to rest the blade in. Brace your thumb to keep the blade in the right spot as you do so. Start making slow steady strokes, keeping your arm properly aligned. Put strength into the push stroke and let up on the pull stroke, but don't overdo it. Let the saw do the work.

5 Once the cut has progressed a few inches, hold the blade at a steeper angle. Long strokes take advantage of the length of the blade. If necessary, use a square or a block of wood to make sure that the saw stays perpendicular to the wood. Support the off-cut as you approach the end, so that it doesn't break off and splinter.

Utility knife

Materials:	**Drywall**
	Cardboard and paper
	Wood
Kits:	**Apartment**
	Home
	Craft
Price:	**$**
Necessity:	**⬡⬡⬡⬡⬡**
Skill level:	**⬡**

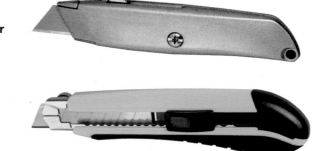

A *utility knife*, also called a *sheet-rock knife*, has a replaceable blade and is used for cutting cardboard boxes, rope or cord, drywall, insulation, etc. The steel blades are thin and trapezoid-shaped, with a cutting edge ground on the base and a notch cut into the top. Half the blade is exposed at any one time. When the exposed cutting edge is worn, the handle is disassembled and the blade flipped over to use the other side. The handle stacks and stores extra blades.

A sliding button on top of the handle moves the blade in or out, and when released, locks it into position. Some knives will only lock the blade in place when fully extended or concealed, others lock the blade at a few points in between.

The handle, made of plastic or metal, is held together with a single screw, and removing the screw to lift off one half of the cover exposes the blade and the sliding mechanism. A bump or bumps engage the notch on the top of the blade, so it is important to note the number of bumps when buying replacement blades.

A utility knife is used frequently so it's worth buying a good one. Look for a sturdy metal or plastic handle, with some reinforcement around the blade opening. Check to ensure the blades slide easily, that they lock firmly into place, and retract completely into the handle.

The knife can be used freehand or with a straightedge. When cutting heavy cardboard or thin plastics, make several light passes rather than trying to cut through in one stroke. When cutting drywall, make one or two passes to score the surface, then flex the board away from the cut to snap along the score line.

Variation:

A *snap-off utility knife* has a long knife blade scored into segments to be snapped off and discarded as the edges dull. Scoring weakens a snap-off blade— they are a good for lighter work.

Hobby knife set

Materials: **Wood**
Kits: **Craft**
Price: **$**
Necessity: ⬡⬡⬡
Skill level: ⬡

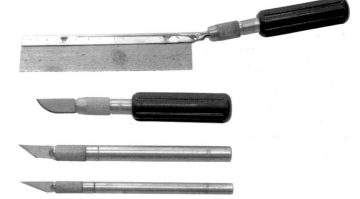

Hobby knives are used for fine work such as model building, graphics, and paper crafts, and very detailed carving and woodworking. They are sometimes called X-acto™ knives—the brand name now being synonymous with their use.

The knives are inexpensive, and have disposable blades that cut with scalpel-like accuracy. A wide range of blade styles are available to fit in three standard handles.

The small- and medium-size handles are held like pencils. They have an aluminum shaft with a knurled barrel surrounding a set of jaws at one end. When the barrel is tightened, the jaws close to grab the blade.

The large handles have a plastic grip similar to a screwdriver and jaws to fit either larger size blades or the frame of especially designed small back saws (see page 74).

Specialized blades and handles are available individually, although it is cost-effective to buy a set of three handles and assorted blades. They can be purchased contained in a small wooden storage box. Larger sets are available outfitted with planes, files, and sanding blocks.

SAFETY FIRST

When you discard a blade, ensure it is wrapped well in cardboard or tape to avoid accidents during garbage disposal.

Glasscutter

Materials: **Glass**
Price: **$**
Necessity: **OOO**
Skill level: **O**

A *glasscutter* doesn't actually cut glass. It scores the surface to enable glass to be broken in a controlled manner. The glass then fractures along the line of weakness created by the score. The cutting action is as if using a knife, with the "blade" of the cutter running along a straightedge.

Glass-cutting tools originally used industrial diamonds glued to the end of a stick. Today, cutters have a small hardened-steel wheel tapering to an edge and mounted in the tip of a metal handle. A series of notches in the side of the handle, above the wheel, and a small ball, are cast onto the opposite end.

The glass must be clean and free of grease and the cutting wheel must be thoroughly lubricated with oil for it to roll, rather than slide on the glass.

Score the full width of the glass and lighten pressure as you reach the end of the cut so you don't chip the edge. Flip the glass over and use the ball on the end of the cutter to gently tap the glass behind the score to weaken it. Flip the glass back over. Flex the glass over a table edge or strip of wood. The glass should break along the score line. If the break is not clean, hook one of the notches in the cutter over the edges to nibble them back to the score line. Use an oilstone to dull the sharp edge of the glass.

A glasscutter works only with plain float glass, which is the glass used in picture frames, mirrors, and older windows. It cannot be used on tempered or laminated glass.

SAFETY FIRST
Always wear eye protection when scoring and snapping glass. Work on a sheet of newspaper to help contain any glass dust or splinters.

Tin snips and aviation shears

Materials: **Sheet metal**
Kits: **Machine and metal work**
Price: **$**
Necessity: **OOO**
Skill level: **O**

Tin snips are large, heavy-duty scissors with short, deep cutting edges. The two handles are attached at a single pivot point. A simple tool, it is available in lengths ranging from 7 to 16 inches. Long handles give good leverage to cut through thick materials. For more control, you can clamp one handle of the snips in a bench vise, allowing you to concentrate on guiding the material through the shears.

Aviation shears evolved from tin snips. They were developed for the aircraft industry to cut tough alloys. They have spring-loaded straight handles, similar to those found on pliers or garden shears. The handles and pivots are designed with an extra link between themand the blades so that the force applied is compounded to make cutting easier.

There are three types, distinguished by colored handles. Yellow indicates a shear capable of making a straight-ahead cut, and cuts to the right or left; red indicates a straight-ahead cut, or a cut to the left; green indicates a straight-ahead cut, or a cut curved to the right. Red- and green-handled shears can cut tighter curves than yellow-handled types.

To cut a tight outside curve or circle with straight-bladed shears or snips, you can nibble away until you achieve the shape you need. For best results, keep the cutting edge of the tool perpendicular to the sheet metal, otherwise the tool can slip sideways and wedge between the cutting jaws, fouling the work and the tool. For the smoothest cut without a ragged edge, don't close the jaws of the shears all the way as you cut. Aviation shears will not cut rods or heavy wire as all the pressure falls on one point, which will crush the rod or wire, not cut it.

When buying these tools, look for smoothly operating shears that have well-forged components.

You can sharpen a used pair of tin snips by clamping them in a vise and filing the edge to an 85° angle.

Diagonal cutters

Materials: **Wire**
Plastic
Kits: **Apartment**
Home
Price: **$**
Necessity: ⬡⬡⬡⬡⬡
Skill level: ⬡

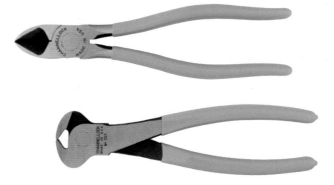

An invaluable tool, these short, sturdy cutters will snip materials, such as wire, cords, thin cable, plastic ties, etc., which would damage the average household scissors. Pliers often have cutters built into them, but they cannot always handle thicker materials. The cutting edges on *diagonal cutters* are curved and offset, allowing the user to snip off a material almost flush with the surrounding surface. Cutters integrated into pliers are often deep in the throat of the tool, while diagonal cutters enable cutting to be carried out in confined spaces.

The tool is simple to use. The most cutting leverage is gained by placing the material as deep into the jaws as possible, but avoid trying to cut anything too thick or too hard. If you force it, you may find this damages the cutting edges.

Variation:
End-cutting pliers can be used in much the same way as diagonal cutters, since the jaws are curved, and grab close to the surface. They are especially useful for pulling staples and finish nails.

TOP TOOL TIP
When pulling finish nails from a piece of trim, use end cutters to pull the nail right through the board and out the back rather than trying to hammer them back out the face. The tips of the cutters let you get a bite on the nail and the curved jaws let you roll the tool to the side, pulling the nail free.

Wire stripper

Materials: **Wire**
Kits: **Electrical**
Price: **$**
Necessity: ❍❍❍
Skill level: ❍

A *wire stripper* is a simple tool with many functions. It looks like a very flat pair of pliers, and has a variety of notches cut into the jaws and handles. The grips on the handles are usually made of insulating material to provide some protection against electric shock from live wires.

A good basic tool will accommodate different wire sizes or gauges generally found around the home.

A wire cutter is situated at the tip of the jaws, and devices further down the jaws are used to crimp electrical connectors. A barrel slides over the end of the wire and is crimp-locked onto the end of the wire.

Additional notches in the handles crimp another type of wire connector. The series of notches closest to the grips strip the insulation casing from the wires, but not the wire inside. Use the numbered notch that corresponds closest to the relevant wire gauge. (See extension cord, page 207, for information on wire gauges.)

A series of holes around the pivot are used to cut screws to a shorter length. To do this, open the jaws until the holes align, poke the screw through, then squeeze the handles to shear the screw.

TOP TOOL TIP
Do not pull insulation straight off wire that is made of many separate strands. Twist it as you slide it off. This will twist the individual strands tightly together, allowing you to make a safer connection.

SAFETY FIRST
Always ensure the power supply to the wiring or device you are working on is shut off before you begin.

Tubing cutter

Materials: **Metal**
Plastic
Kits: **Plumbing**
Price: **$**
Necessity: **OOO**
Skill level: **O**

A *tubing cutter* is used to cut through copper, PVC, steel, brass and aluminum tubing, and pipe. Several sizes of cutter are available to accommodate everything from small brake line tubing right up to pipe that is several inches in diameter.

All types of cutters operate on the same principle: a hardened-steel cutting wheel is held across from a pair of rollers inside a C-shaped steel frame. The pipe is placed between the cutter and the rollers. Turning the knob on the end of the tool, clamps the pipe between the two.

Once the pipe is in place, the knob is turned to apply pressure to the pipe. With the knob held tight, the entire tool spins to roll the cutting wheel around the circumference of a pipe. It is then rotated once in the opposite direction to achieve a clean score. As the cutter scores the pipe, the tool becomes easier to move, and the knob is tightened again. There should be a moderate level of resistance when spinning the tool around the pipe.

As the tool spins easily again, so the knob is tightened until the cutting wheel cuts deeper. The process is repeated until the wheel cuts all the way through the wall of the pipe.

In most tubing cutters, a triangular piece of metal, called a reamer, flips or slides out of the tool's frame. Poke the tip of the reamer into the freshly cut end of the tube and twist it back and forth to burnish the edge and smooth out any burrs.

Handsaw

Materials: **Wood**
Kits: **Apartment**
Home
Price: **$**
Necessity: **OOOO**
Skill level: **OO**

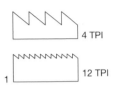

4 TPI

1   12 TPI

To understand how a saw works, you need to know that a piece of wood is a bundle of very fine tubes, forming the "grain." Saws used for cutting wood divide into three categories depending on whether they are used to cut parallel to the grain (a ripsaw), across the grain (a crosscut saw) or whether they are suitable for either cutting method (combination saw).

The angle, number, and shape of its teeth are what make a saw suitable for a particular cut. Their size determines how quickly the cut will be achieved and how smooth the finish will look. "Teeth per inch" or TPI, measures the fineness of a saw's teeth. A saw intended for rough cuts has fewer, larger teeth and a lower TPI than a saw intended for fine cuts (*see figure 1*).

A crosscut saw's teeth are shaped like little knife tips with their edges sharpened and beveled toward the center of the blade. A ripsaw's teeth are shaped like a row of chisels and are only sharp on their leading edge.

Saw teeth are bent, or "set," out to one side or the other slightly, alternating tooth by tooth down the length of the saw blade. This is to make the kerf wider than the blade of the saw.

Handsaws are good for large, rough cuts. If you need to do significant amounts of rip cutting, you may want to invest in a table saw, but if you are cutting only a few pieces, a hand ripsaw is the more compact option. For a beginner, it usually makes sense to buy a crosscut saw first and add a ripsaw later. A combination saw gives acceptable results for either cut.

Older saw blades are "taper ground" and thinner toward the front and top of the blade, making it less likely to bind. Made of soft steel, they can be repeatedly sharpened. Contemporary saws are made of rolled, hardened steel, to the same thickness all the way through. This enables the teeth to hold an edge for much longer, but once they are dull, they are almost impossible to sharpen.

Back saw

Materials: **Wood**
Plastic
Metal
Price: **$**
Necessity: ⬡⬡⬡
Skill level: ⬡

Back saws are specialized handsaws. The blade is rectangular in shape, with a brass or steel spine running along the top edge to keep it rigid. The spine may be composed of metal folded and clamped over the blade, or it may be a solid bar with a slot milled into it. With their small teeth and added rigidity, back saws are used to make fine, precise cuts for millwork and joinery.

They are available in rip, crosscut, and combination teeth configurations. While the spine gives added stiffness, it does limit the depth of the cut you can make, because once you go deep, it will get in the way.

Small back saws, also called *gent's saws* or *dovetail saws*, are shorter and have around 25 TPI (teeth per inch, see page 73). These are used for cutting joint components like tenons and dovetails. Unlike larger back saws with a pistol-style or D-shaped handle, the handles of dovetail saws are made of a single, turned

piece of hardwood sticking straight out from the end of the spine. They are available as both rip and crosscut saws. Cuts parallel with the grain are more common though, so if you had to choose one, go with the rip-style teeth.

Very fine back saws, a few inches long and with as many as 52 TPI, are available for very detailed work, such as model building. They are usually available from hobby knife manufacturers, and are used in conjunction with large knife handles.

Large back saws are often used in conjunction with a miter box to cut materials at an angle. These have 14 to 22 TPI and are usually sold as a crosscut style saw. Small miter boxes are also available.

Japanese handsaw

Materials: **Wood**
Price: **$$**
Necessity: ○○
Skill level: ○○○

Japanese handsaws have a loyal following among experienced woodworkers. They can be expensive, and good-quality ones must be shipped to a specialist for sharpening. The main difference between a Japanese handsaw and European is that the cut in the Japanese saw is performed on the pull stroke rather than the push, and its much thinner blade, made from hard steel, holds an edge extremely well. The narrow blade means the saw removes less wood, and this, coupled with sharp teeth, makes for a quick, smooth cut. However, even though the saw is flexible, the metal is brittle and the teeth are easily damaged if treated carelessly or used roughly in hard woods. They are best suited for use with soft woods.

The handle of a Japanese saw is long and slim, extending out from the heel of the blade. This allows you to hold the handle with both hands for better control. Many more reasonably priced saws are designed to be disposed of once they dull or are damaged. Some have reusable handles or replaceable blades. When not in use, the saws must be wrapped in canvas with a light coating of camellia oil to prevent tarnishing.

Categories:

Kataba: has a single cutting edge on the blade and may be either ripsaw or crosscut saw.

Ryoba: has teeth on both edges of the blade. One side for rip cuts, one for cross cuts. Saws for fine work are 7½ to 9 inches long; 10¾ to 11½ inch saws are for heavier carpentry.

Dozuki: meaning "shoulder." Tooth patterns and blade thickness vary depending on the type of cut and wood.

Kugihiki: meaning "to cut nails." This short flexible saw will trim wood pins and dowels flush with surrounding wood. The blades can bend flat on a board's surface and because the teeth have no set, they will not scratch the wood.

Miter saw and box

Materials: **Wood**
Price: **$–$$$**
Necessity: **○○**
Skill level: **○○**

A *miter saw* is a highly accurate hand tool used for precisely angled cuts. It consists of a saw permanently built into a frame that is able to rotate horizontally through a wide range of angles while holding the saw perpendicular to the base. The blade remains perfectly aligned as it cuts through the wood, delivering a clean, accurate cut. Some saw frames also tip to the side to make a bevel cut at an angle, which is useful when working with intricate moldings. Many of the powered miter saws available share this feature (see page 88).

A *miter box* is a ready-made jig used to hold the miter saw at a predetermined angle. It consists of a U-shaped wood, metal, or plastic channel with slots in the walls in which the blade rides. The material for cutting lies in the bottom of the box, against the far wall.

Simple miter boxes have slots to hold the saw at 90° and 45° to the material in the box, providing an accurate and consistent square and miter cut.

Miter trimmer

Materials: **Wood**
Price: **$$**
Necessity: **OO**
Skill level: **OO**

1

A *miter trimmer* is designed to help make precise, glass-smooth angle cuts in molding and other pieces of wood, such as those used in picture framing.

It is a horizontal guillotine in a heavy steel frame. Stops at either end hold the wood at a preset angle. A lever is pulled to advance a large steel blade to pare off the end of the wood. First, the wood to be trimmed is cut with a saw within ⅛ inch or so of the final cut line. The miter trimmer slices off the remaining wood.

The miter trimmer has evolved from the *shooting board*, a much simpler, home-made mechanism, and essentially a jig that guides the action of a hand plane.

The plane is placed on its side and moved back and forth, like the blade in the miter trimmer. A stop screws to the jig at a 45° angle to the guide edge, providing a lip to hold the work piece (*see figure 1*). To work properly, the plane must be in good order, and its blade should be sharp and set parallel to the sole.

Compass saw

Materials: **Wood**
Drywall
Price: **$**
Necessity: OOOO
Skill level: OO

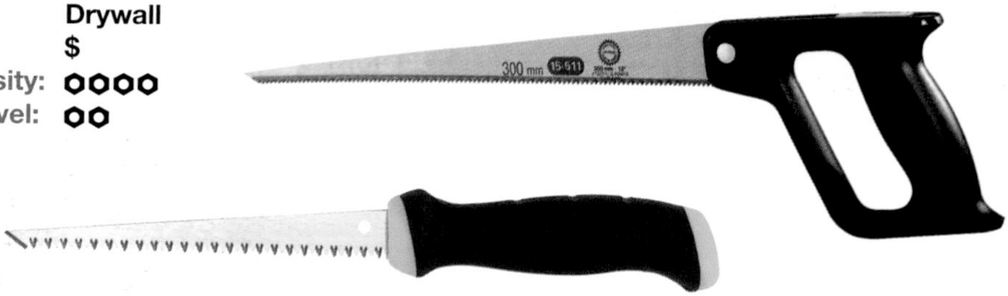

Compass saws, or keyhole saws, are short, narrow saws with a pistol-style handle and a blade that tapers to a point at the end. Often, there are a few interchangeable blades clamped into the handle. Their thinness allows the cutting of curves that a coping saw (see page 80) cannot reach, or to make cuts in the interior of a work piece or fitting.

First an access hole is drilled into the cutting area, large enough to slip the tip of the saw in and begin the cut. It's best to cut out the waste in a few pieces for easier maneuvering of the saw. Large curved cuts or interior cuts are usually done with a saber saw, but there are still occasions when a handsaw is an easier tool to use. A modern alternative is a handle for either a saber saw or reciprocating saw blade, which gives a wide range of blade choices. A mini hacksaw handle will do the same for hacksaw blades.

The punch saw is designed for cutting drywall. When instaling drywall, you need to make cutouts in the sheet to accommodate electrical outlets, switches, lighting, etc. The punch saw has a narrow, pointed blade, about ⅛ inch thick, with aggressive teeth. A large rubber handle provides a sound grip so the tip of the saw can be punched into the center of the area to be cut out, and the blade's thickness prevents it from bending during the action.

Hacksaw

Materials:	**Metal**
Kits:	**Machine and metal work**
Price:	**$**
Necessity:	**OOOO**
Skill level:	**O**

1

The *hacksaw* is one of the few frame-type saws still in common use. A thin, flexible steel blade with fine hardened teeth is held in tension by a rigid steel frame. The frame has a pistol or D-shaped handle and can be adjusted to accommodate differing length blades. The blade is held at either end by hook-shaped pieces called *spigots* which fit into holes in the blade. One of them has a wing nut to adjust the tension on the blade. If the blade is too loose, it won't stay straight and may break. If it's too tight, it will start to warp.

Look for a sturdy frame that also has a comfortable handle. Small blade handles are available to clamp on one end of the blade, making it into a keyhole saw of sorts. These work well for small cuts or to slip the tip of the saw blade into a slot. They are easy to toss in a toolbox and are a good way to get some extra life out of a broken or partially dull blade.

Blades range in coarseness from 14 to 32 TPI (teeth per inch, see page 73).

Coarse blades are used for soft metals like brass or aluminum. Fine blades tend to clog on these materials, and are better suited to thin, hard materials. Bar, tubing, bolts, pipes, and sheet stock can all be cut with a hacksaw.

TOP TOOL TIPS
• Clamp the work piece in a vise to prevent it from moving around. Metal pieces can get hot, so use the vise instead of your hands to hold them.
• When cutting pipe or tubing, rotate the tube, using the hacksaw to cut one wall at a time (*see figure 1*).
• When cutting thick stock, cut along each face first, then cut through the remainder to make sure of a square cut.
• Before cutting a bolt or threaded rod, first thread on a couple of nuts. Close the vise on the nuts instead of the bolt or rod to prevent mashing the threads. Remove the nuts after the cut to help straighten any threads damaged by sawing.

Coping saw

Materials: **Wood**
Plastic
Price: **$**
Necessity: **OOO**
Skill level: **OO**

1

A *coping saw* has a slim, fine-toothed blade that hooks into a spigot on each end of a U-shaped steel frame. Twisting the handle, which is threaded onto one of the spigots, tensions the frame and blade.

Coping saws make small, fine cuts and tight curved cuts in wood and plastic. They are used to cut patterns or cleat waste from dovetail joints. It is named a coping saw because it "copes" pieces of wood together to achieve a tight joint between, for example, two pieces of molding meeting at less than 90°. Rather than cut both pieces at an angle, one is run into the corner and its profile is cut out of the other.

The blades are about 6 inches long and typically have 14 to 32 TPI (see page 73). Because there is so little depth to the blade, it's easy to make the cut curve. The throat of the frame limits the depth of cut, but the spigots that hold the blade can be turned to point in any direction.

The blades will cut on the push or the pull. When working on a piece clamped in a vise, either way will work. When working material clamped to a bench, set the blade to cut on the pull stroke. Hold the saw handle below the work piece, and when you make the stroke the work is pulled down onto the support, instead of up off it (*see figure 1*). Use this to your advantage when working with small or thin pieces by making a jig known as a "bird's mouth," a board with a V-shaped notch cut into the end and clamped to the edge of the workbench. By keeping the blade of the saw in the base of the V, the wood around the cut is well-supported, yet free to be twisted to make intricate cuts.

Variations:
Fret saw will cut curves finer and tighter than a coping saw. The frame has a much deeper throat, to accommodate larger work pieces.

Piercing saw uses the finest blades in this family—up to 80 TPI—for delicate cuts in thin sheet metal, such as jewelry work.

Jigsaw

Materials: **Wood**
Metal
Plastic
Drywall
Price: **$**
Necessity: **OOOO**
Skill level: **OO**

In the family of handheld electric saws, the *jigsaw*, sometimes called a *saber saw*, is the jack-of-all-trades, and for beginners to power saws, more comfortable than some of its brawnier cousins.

The handheld jigsaw travels on top of a work piece on a flat base plate. The motor and blade assembly is mounted on top of the plate. The blade extends down through the base plate and travels up and down, either cycling in a straight line, which is the reciprocating movement, or on an elliptical path, called an orbital movement.

In an orbital movement, the blade moves away from the cut edge on the downstroke and toward it on the upstroke. This method cuts faster and causes less wear on the blade, but tends to splinter the surface of the work piece.

A reciprocating movement works better when appearance counts more than speed. High-quality saws provide the opportunity to select either type of movement.

The jigsaw makes straight cuts, curved, and angled cuts, and with the addition of a jig allowing the saw to pivot around a center, it cuts near-perfect circles. Some saws have a scrolling feature to cut tighter curves. By releasing a lock, and turning a knob on top of the saw, the blade quickly pivots 360°.

The jigsaw really shines when making cuts in the interior of a flat surface, like cutting a hole in a countertop to fit a sink. To make this type of cut, first drill an access hole in each corner of the opening, and use the saw to connect the dots.

Different blade speeds and types are suitable for different materials. A good saw allows you to vary the speed of the blade. Some models have different blade-holding mechanisms for hooked, straight, or barbed blade shapes, and a quick-release blade system is a nice feature if you use the tool frequently.

Reciprocating saw

Materials: **Wood**
Metal
Plastic
Plaster
Drywall
Roofing
Price: **$$$**
Necessity: **OOO**
Skill level: **OOO**

A *reciprocating saw* is like an electric jigsaw on steroids! It's the tool of choice for performing selective demolition and rough utility and plumbing installation, because with the right blade, it can cut through just about anything—framing lumber, metal and plastic pipe, drywall and roofing. You can jab it into a starter hole and cut through plaster, lath, and framing studs and siding to make a new opening for a window or door, without any surrounding damage. Reciprocating saws are also known as *sawzalls*, a generic name taken from the Milwaukee Electric Tool Corp's branding first introduced in the 1950s.

A motor housing has a D-shaped handle with a trigger switch on one end. At the opposite end it tapers and holds a blade mount and a pivoting foot. The saw is held like a sawn-off shotgun, one hand on the handle, the other above the blade housing.

Like jigsaws, reciprocating saws operate in reciprocating or orbiting motion.

Orbiting is more aggressive, but the smoother, reciprocating motion works better for hard materials, such as metal pipes. Some models offer the option of selecting either, and high-end models usually incorporate an internal counter-balance to minimize vibration.

Different blades are available: most are bi-metal blades with hardened-steel teeth that are attached to a flexible steel blade. Depending on the work, one part of the blade may wear quicker than another part, and to extend the life of a blade, many saws have a foot that moves the blade to another fresh section of teeth.

Cordless models are best suited for lighter jobs and shorter run times.

SAFETY FIRST

Because these saws are often used when making rough cuts in awkward positions, gloves and eye protection are always to be recommended.

Scroll saw

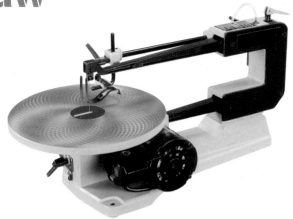

Materials: **Wood**
Metal
Plastic
Glass
Ceramic
Price: **$$$**
Necessity: **OO**
Skill level: **OO**

Scroll saws are the powered cousin of the coping saw—they work faster (500 to 1,500 strokes per minute versus 60). Veneer and inlay projects, fretwork, and jewelry work are done on a scroll saw.

The blade oscillates up and down in a fixed position in the center of a support table, leaving both hands free to move the work piece through the saw. Treadle-powered, and later electric, models were once connected to a separate motor via a belt. Current models have small motors built right into the saw's body.

The saw is built around a C-shaped frame, which has a blade held taut between its open ends. Modern frames may pivot up and down as one piece, or the top and bottom legs may pivot parallel to each other.

A range of blades available gives the scroll saw great versatility. Blades with fine teeth are suitable for cutting thin or hard materials. Coarser blades work better with thick or soft materials. Blade speed,

alignment, and tension also are important, and the combinations vary depending on the material and the intricacy of the cut. Slow speeds are for thin, delicate cuts, medium speeds for thick or tough material, and fast speeds are for quick, rough cuts or hard materials.

Look for a well-built machine with a good-sized table and a throat that is deep enough to accommodate your work. Tilting tables should move smoothly and lock into place accurately. The machine should have very little vibration for best results. Check how easy it is to adjust the saw's speed and how easy it is to change the blade.

Band saw

Materials: **Wood**
Metal
Plastic
Price: **$$$–$$$$**
Necessity: **OO**
Skill level: **OO**

If you are starting to woodwork in a home shop, a *band saw* might be one of the first large tools you purchase. It is safe, quiet, compact, generates less dust than a table saw (see page 90), and is versatile. It rip cuts, cross cuts, cuts curves and angles, and can slice a long board into narrower strips, cut away waste in joinery, and curve and profile parts for furniture and other projects.

The saw is built around a C-shaped frame made from cast iron, or steel, or welded sheet metal. The blade fits over large pulleys housed behind covers at the top and bottom of the frame. It runs up through the back of the frame over the top pulley, out through the open part of the frame, through a hole in the table and down around the bottom pulley.

The blade is the key to the saw's design. It operates in a continuous loop, so it can continue moving in the cutting direction. There are blade guides above and below the table to prevent it from flexing or wandering. The upper guide slides to accommodate materials of different thickness. A motor sits outboard of the saw and drives the lower pulley. A fence clamps to rails on the edge of the table so your work remains aligned with the blade. Slots milled into the table accept a miter square that allows the accurate movement of stock perpendicular to the blade. A pivoting assembly on the bottom of the table allows it to tilt for angled cuts.

The size of the pulleys determines the maximum width of the material you can saw. The diameter of the pulley is roughly equal to the depth of the frame's throat. Saws are available with wheels that are 8, 12, 14, 16, 24, and 36 inches. Eight- and 12-inch saws are light-duty hobbyist models bolted to a bench top. Mid-size saws are typically found in the workshops of serious amateur as well as professional woodworkers.

Round saw blades

Materials: **Wood**
Metal
Masonry
Plastic
Price: **$-$$**
Necessity: **OOO**
Skill level: **OOO**

Using a *round saw blade* is like having an infinitely long saw, because there is no beginning or end to it. They are most commonly used in circular saws, table saws and miter saws. They all look the same, but several factors make a particular blade better suited for one task or another.

Size: Different types of saws use different size blades.

Shape of the teeth: There are three differing cutting edges:
• Flat top, or FT—the tops of the teeth are ground straight across like a rip saw.
• Alternate top bevel, or ATB—every other tooth is ground at an angle toward the center of the blade, like a crosscut saw.
• Triple chip, TC—similar to the FT, but every other tooth has its top corners beveled off and the heights of the teeth alternate. This edge performs well on plastics, and hard, manmade materials.

Number of teeth: Fewer teeth give a fast, rough cut; more teeth give a slower but smoother cut.

Hook angle: A tooth angled toward the cut, is a positive tooth angle; when it angles away from the cut, it is known as negative. Teeth with a steep, positive angle provide a more aggressive cut. Shallow angles offer smoother cuts and are better suited to dense materials.

Material: Lower-quality saw blades are made from ground and sharpened steel. They are adequate, but it is well worth upgrading to high-quality, carbide-tipped blades, which are mostly made of steel, but have cutting teeth of tungsten carbide, a strong, hard, heat-resistant ceramic. These carbide tips are brazed onto the blade's steel body. They are more durable and hold an edge longer; the tips are wider than the body, which makes the blade less likely to bind in the cut. There also are

Continued 85

abrasive and diamond blades for more specialized applications.

Thin kerf rip blade: A steep hook angle, deep gullets, and few, flat top ground teeth are the marks of a thin kerf rip blade. These blades are thinner than standard ones. As a result, there is less wood lost to the cut and less work for the saw.

Combination blade: A large number of alternating ATB teeth and FT teeth, and a shallow hook angle will deliver smooth clean results on both cross and rip cuts. Note the expansion slots cut into the rim, which help reduce noise and vibration.

Abrasive blades: Used in chop saws and miter saws to cut ferrous and non-ferrous metals. These blades are available in different grits for different tasks,and are made from resin-bonded aluminum oxide or silicon carbide.

Diamond blades: Used to cut masonry, tile, stone, and concrete. Diamond grit is soldered or laser-welded to the rim of the blade. The rim may be segmented or continuous. Some blades must be flushed with water during use to clean the kerf, cool the blade, and allow for deeper cuts. Others can be used dry, but take care to avoid overheating.

Dado: The dado set is used in a table saw to cut a long, continuous groove in a piece of wood, known as a dado. The set consists of a pair of outer blades and a group of splitters, which are sandwiched between the blades. By assembling combinations of blades and splitters, you can cut dados from $1/4$ to $13/16$ inches in width. Ten-inch table saws use 8-inch diameter dado sets; 8-inch saws use 6-inch sets.

Circular saw

Materials: **Wood**
Metal
Price: **$$–$$$**
Necessity: **OOOO**
Skill level: **OOO**

The *circular saw* long ago overtook the handsaw as the tool for cutting framing lumber and sheet goods. It is a good investment if you are planning a major renovation or a fair-sized carpentry project.

Circular saws are available in two configurations—*worm drives* and *sidewinders*. A worm drive has the centerline of its motor parallel to the blade. This configuration is favored for the high torque and durability. More common though, is the sidewinder, where the shaft of the motor is perpendicular to the blade. Sidewinders are lighter, more compact, less expensive, and will require less maintenance than their beefier cousins. Both styles usually use 7¼-inch blades.

The motor and blade assembly has a D-shaped handle with a trigger switch at the rear and a knob at the front so that the saw can be held with two hands. The top half of the blade is covered by a fixed guard. A spring-loaded retractable guard covers the bottom half and gets pushed out of the way as the saw proceeds through the cut. It flips back into place once the blade clears the kerf.

The motor and blade assembly is attached to a broad base plate called a table or sole. The two parts are connected with a pivot on the leading edge of the sole, which lets you raise and lower the blade through a slot within it. A lever on the side locks the blade to the desired height. The sole is also able to pivot side to side so that the saw can make beveled cuts.

The quality of a circular saw's sole points to its accuracy, and the best saws have soles of reinforced cast alloy or heavy-duty plastic.

The blade is attached with a single nut at its center, which is called an arbor nut. Before changing or replacing the blade, make sure it's unplugged. The blade must be held in place so it cannot turn before it can be removed. Some saws have a button to press, which will lock it in place.

Powered miter saw

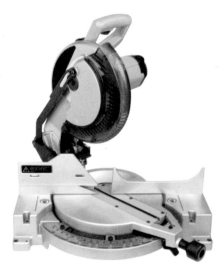

Materials: **Wood**
Metal
Price: **$$$–$$$$**
Necessity: **OO**
Skill level: **OO**

The *powered miter saw*, or *chop saw*, makes angled, or mitered, crosscuts. Its round, motorized blade is mounted on a spring-loaded pivoting arm that is attached to a small cast steel or aluminum base and has a fence running along its back edge.

Most miter saws operate by pivoting the cutting blade down onto a work piece. held against the fence. A retractable guard moves out of the way as the cut is made. Blades range in size from 8 to 15 inches. A 10-inch blade, for example, easily makes a 90° cut through a 4 x 4-inch post but would not make it all the way through a 2 x 8-inch post. Blades vary to suit fast, rough cuts for framing, or fine, smooth cuts for finish work or for tough materials like metal studs and pipe.

The simplest miter saws are *cutoff saws*, which cut 90° angles. They are usually fitted with abrasive blades to cut pipe or metal stock to length.

Basic miter saws are next in line. The arm housing the motor and blade is mounted on a turntable that can pivot on the base. Most will allow the blade to pivot 45° to the left and right of center with calibrated stops to lock the blade at commonly used angles.

A *compound miter saw's* blade not only pivots left to right, it lies down one side to make a bevel cut. The bevel cut allows an angled cut to be made across a wide board. The *sliding compound miter saw* can make miter and bevel cuts, with the difference that the blade and motor assembly are attached to a rail, allowing the blade to move horizontally across the work piece. This means cutting capacity is not tied to the size of the blade, making wider cuts possible.

A miter saw or compound miter saw with a 10-inch blade will suit a beginner.

The *sliding dual compound miter saw* is the Cadillac of miter saws. It is larger, heavier and the most expensive.

Radial arm saw

Materials: **Wood**
Price: **$$**
Necessity: **OO**
Skill level: **OO**

Radial arm saws are a dying breed. Once a common fixture in real enthusiasts' home workshops, their use has been usurped by the portable miter saw (see page 88). Though not transportable, the radial saw is useful because the width of its cut is not dependent on the diameter of the blade, and it can cut material a foot or more across in width.

The radial arm saw is built around a sturdy vertical post with an arm that extends out from the top of it. A yoke holding a type of circular saw hangs from the bottom of the arm and is free to slide back and forth. The bottom of the post is mounted to the top of a long, shallow counter or bench, which is built up against a wall. A stop is built along the back edge of the bench so the material to be cut has a resting place and the saw is aligned so that it cuts perpendicular to the stop.

The radial arm saw does have some flexibility. The yoke pivots on the arm to make bevel cuts, and you can raise the height of the entire saw and install a dado blade (see page 86). Sanding and drilling attachments are available for the tool, but dedicated machines accomplish the job better and do not require the setup time that is involved in converting the saw to another use. Consequently, the tool always remained mainly a cutoff saw.

Due to the danger associated with bevel cutting and ripping operations, it is a good idea to purchase professional training if you plan to include a radial arm saw in your workshop.

Table saw

Materials: **Wood**
             Plastic
Price: **$$$$**
Necessity: **OOO**
Skill level: **OOO**

All *table saws* have a circular, motorized blade that can be raised and lowered through a slot in a cast metal table that is almost perfectly flat. Sliding on rails mounted on the front and rear of the table is a fence that moves left and right, parallel to the blade. It can be locked into position at a desired distance from the blade in order to align the board as it is pushed through the saw. This ensures the cut is straight and the board is a consistent width throughout (*see figures 1 and 2*).

The long fence and broad table makes the table saw ideal for long, straight cuts, but plenty of space is needed to accommodate the material. A table saw excels at rip cuts. With store-bought or homemade jigs, the saw can also be used to make more complex cuts, such as for tenons, box and dovetail joints, even a cove in the face of a board. By setting the blade height so that it doesn't cut all the way through the material, the blade will cut grooves, called dados.

The table sits on a metal or plastic base on which are mounted the saw's control mechanisms. Hand cranks raise and lower the blade and tilt it sideways. These cranks twist and pivot a stout metal casting inside the base called the trunion. The trunion carries the motor, the blade, and the belt drive system connecting the two, and allows them to move as one unit.

The blade is attached to the trunion by the arbor and it is held in place by the arbor nut. This nut has to be removed to change the blade. To make this easier, there is an oval-shaped panel in the center of the table called the throat plate, which when removed allows access the arbor nut and the blade.

Safety devices cover the blade to protect against kickback. The best way to avoid kickback is to hold the material securely against both the table and the fence and plan so cutoff material doesn't get trapped between the fence and blade. Never freehand cut on a table saw.

3

The smallest and lightest is the *portable table saw*. Compact enough to be toted around and tossed back in the truck at the end of the day, they have no legs and must be set up on sawhorses or a workbench.

While the lighter weight may be easier on your back, it doesn't help the quality of the saw's cut. Weight is a table saw's friend. It dampens the vibrations that make it difficult to get a smooth cut.

A *contractor's saw*, while still considered "portable," does take two to carry. They are popular for their increased weight, better motors and cast iron tables, which often have iron or sheet-metal "wings" that bolt to the table edge and offer additional working surface. The saws have a sheet metal base cabinet with legs that allow it to stand free.

Cabinet saws are the saws of choice for serious hobbyist woodworkers. They have strong motors, broad, heavy tables and added mass in the base and trunion which further damps vibration and makes

for a solid machine. The entire base, from floor to table, is enclosed, forming a large cabinet that houses the motor and trunion. This also helps to contain the sawdust, which is removed from the cabinet through a trap door in its side.

Hybrid saws combine the smaller table and the legs of a contractor's saw with the enclosed motor and base and broader footprint of a cabinet style saw. They are priced to be competitive with contractor's saws, at about half the cost of the cheapest cabinet saws.

There are several accessories to the table saw. A face shield should be worn at all times when using the saw. Hearing protection is also recommended. As you feed stock through the saw, use push sticks to keep your fingers away from the blade.

An out-feed support, which is a simple, adjustable stand with a roller top (*see figure 3*), should be used to hold the stock as it slides out the back end of the saw.

Making holes

The drilling or cutting of holes is most often required to accommodate fasteners, such as bolts or screws, needed for fixtures and fittings. Sometimes a drilled hole is a starting point to saw a larger cut-out in a work piece. Hole-making tools make openings in all sizes and materials, and with varying degrees of accuracy, and for each, there are some basic principles to keep in mind for safety, for efficiency and for better results.

General rules
- Place or clamp a scrap piece of wood beneath or behind the work to prevent splintering when the bit emerges. This will also protect the work surface.

- Be sure the work piece is securely held in place, especially when drilling into the end or edge of a board. If necessary, make a jig to hold odd-shaped pieces.

- Use the right bit for the material and for the hole size and type.

Beginner's class

To drill a hole, the first step is to mark its location on your work piece. If you have multiple holes to make, it is most efficient to do all the layout work at once.

1 Use an awl or center punch to mark the center of hole. This makes a little divot for the tip of the drill bit to rest in, which helps keep it accurately located and prevents it slipping to the side as you begin to drill.

2 If the work piece is small, clamp it to the bench top or hold it securely in a vise. If you

intend to drill all of the way through the material, place a piece of scrap wood beneath the hole to avoid drilling into the bench. This will also keep the bottom surface of the work piece from splintering as the bit emerges.

3 Select a drill and bit based on the size and depth of the hole, the material you'll be drilling into and, if applicable, the type of fastener that will be used in the hole. (See page 94 for more on bits and page 164 for more on fasteners.)

Insert the bit into the chuck of the drill and tighten it so that the bit is held securely. (See page 97 for more on chucks.)

- Use an awl or punch to mark the center of the hole before you drill.

- For best results, use a sharp bit. If it is dull, replace it or sharpen it using a file or a commercially available bit sharpener.

- Ensure the bit is securely clamped into the chuck.

- Hold the tool perpendicular to the surface to be drilled. Use a square or block of wood for comparison.

- Wear eye protection. Make sure hair, clothing, and jewelry are pulled back and secured to avoid snagging or tangling.

- Don't advance the bit too quickly. When drilling hard or brittle material like plastic, it is helpful to start the hole with a small bit and work up to the final size bit.

- When the depth of a hole is critical, use a depth stop (a sleeve clamped around the bit), or improvize by wrapping a piece of tape around the bit to mark where to stop drilling.

- Drill bits can get hot during drilling, especially if they are dull or if you are making a large hole. Back the drill out of the hole periodically to help eject shavings and allow the bit to cool.

4 Place the tip of the drill bit on the center mark that you made with the awl and hold the drill so the bit is perpendicular to the work surface. From whatever direction you look at it, it should not look tipped. If it does, the hole will be made through 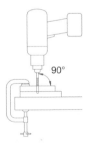 the work piece at a skewed angle. You may want to use a square block of wood to compare against or to have a helper "spot" you and tell you if the bit is straight.

5 Most electric drills have a variable speed trigger which works like the gas pedal on a car— the harder you press the faster it goes. As you start drilling, the motor should run relatively slowly. Once the hole is established, you can increase the speed.

When the hole reaches full depth, keep the motor running and pull the bit from the hole. Don't stop the drill with the bit in the hole, it may bind, and be tough to remove.

With that, the hole is complete and you are ready to move onto the next step.

Drill bits

Materials:	**Wood**
	Metal
	Plastic
	Glass
	Ceramic
Kits:	**Home**
Price:	**$**
Necessity:	**OOO**
Skill level:	**OO**

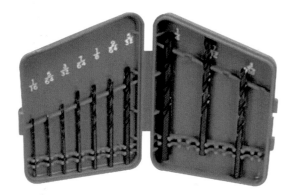

A drill must have a bit installed to function as a hole making instrument. There are many types, and all tailored to specific materials, hole sizes, and quality of finish. The most common types are described. *Twist and brad point bits* can only be used in hand-powered drills, but all those included can be used with electric drills.

It is easiest to buy drill bits in sets that include a range of sizes. The bits can also then be purchased individually if one should dull, break or be lost.

Twist bits: The most commonly used—they are good, general-purpose bits—they are inexpensive, easy to sharpen, and they work on a wide variety of materials, including wood, metal, and plastic. Spiral flutes twist up the shank of the bit in order to disperse wood chips away from the two cutting edges ground on the tip. The edges are ground at 60°, but are some-times ground to a more acute point. This offsets a twist bit's tendency to slip off the

mark at the start of drilling. When accuracy is important, an awl (see page 54) will mark the center to enable a more efficient start.

Brad point bits: Look much like a twist bit but with a center point built into the tip of the drill. The point grabs the wood and keeps the bit centered as the cutting edges begin to drill into wood, or plastic. This makes it easier to precisely locate holes, and enables successful drilling of holes at an angle as the point gives the bit a foothold on the material.

There are two types: spurred and unspurred. A spurred bit gives a much cleaner hole than either the twist bit or the unspurred version, though it is a little trickier to sharpen.

Masonry bits: Have spiral chip-clearing flutes, and hardened steel or carbide cutters brazed onto the tip. Though not especially sharp, they are hard enough to maintain their edge while cutting through

hard masonry, such as concrete, block, brick, limestone, or bluestone.

Spade bits: Small and inexpensive, they make fast work of drilling holes from ¼ to 1½ inches in diameter into wood. The tip of the spade bit is similar to a large brad point, except the point, spurs, and cutting edges are ground into a flat piece of steel, attached to a long, slim shank.

The spade bit has an especially long center point that will burrow into a bench top before the bit gets through the wood. If you intend to drill through the work piece, keep in mind the center point will exit the bottom of the piece first. A piece of scrap underneath will avoid damaging the work surface and minimize tearout. Once the tip emerges from the bottom, flip the work over and complete the hole from that side.

Forstner bits: Excel at drilling on steep angles and leaves a clean, flat-bottomed hole, and is used on wood. The bit is commonly available in sizes from ¼ to 2 inches and delivers best results when used in a drill press. But it does have a couple of drawbacks in that while its wide rim helps keep the bit tracking straight, it does not clear chips well, and it generates a lot of heat from friction. Too much heat can ruin a bit's ability to hold an edge and cause burn marks on a work piece. When drilling deep holes, do a little at a time and blow the chips out as you go. If you are making several holes, pause occasionally to allow the bit to cool.

Glass and tile bits: These bits have an arrowhead tip designed for drilling through brittle materials, such as glass, ceramic, and terra cotta tiles. It is the bit to use when mounting fixtures in a tiled bathroom or kitchen.

Hole saw

Materials: **Wood**
Plastic
Price: **$**
Necessity: **OOO**
Skill level: **OO**

Consider the edge of a hole as a circle—a regular drill bit works by chewing away everything inside that circle and shredding it to dust. When making big holes, this takes a lot of time and effort and generates a lot of heat that can damage a bit. The *hole saw* works more efficiently to drill large holes.

The saw consists of a steel cup with hardened teeth on its rim. A special pilot bit called a *mandrel* passes through the center of the cup and locks in place. The end of the mandrel is chucked into an electric drill, enabling it to spin both the saw and the pilot bit. This bit bores into the wood a little ahead of the saw, which accurately locates the hole and keeps the saw spinning around a consistent center. (One mandrel can interchange between several different saws.)

As the hole saw spins, the teeth on its edge follow each other around and around the edge of the circle, cutting deeper and deeper until they cut all the way through.

This leaves a large hole in the work piece and a disc of material being cut away inside the cup of the saw.

Hole saws cut the holes required to install a lock set in a door or to install wire grommets in a desk or countertop, and can be used on wood or plastic

Circle cutters are similar to hole saws in that they also cut away the edge of a hole. Like the hole saw, they have a center mandrel that is held by a drill's chuck.

Instead of using a cup-shaped saw with many teeth, they use a single cutting tooth that is attached to the end of an adjustable arm which passes through the mandrel. The arm allows the cutting tooth to be moved in or out, to drill holes of a variety of radii with a single tool. The drawback is that the circle cutter will deliver poor results when used in a handheld electric drill, so it should only be used in a drill press.

Chuck

Materials: **Wood**
Metal
Plastic
Glass
Ceramic
Kits: **Home**
Price: **$**
Necessity: **OOOO**
Skill level: **O**

A *chuck* is the clamp-like device on the end of a drill that holds the bit or cutting tool in the drill head. Most are built around a steel sleeve, which is tapered on the inside. Within the sleeve and visible through the hole in the end are two, three, or four jaws, depending on the chuck. When the sleeve is turned, the jaws wedge into the tapered end, pushing together, and this pressure holds the bit in place.

It is important the bit is centered in the chuck so that it can be grabbed by all of the jaws. If not, when the drill is activated the bit will wobble around the center point, possibly damaging the bit, the work piece, and the jaws of the chuck.

Most corded electric drills, drill presses, and some cordless drills use a small-geared chuck key. Turning the key draws the jaws down tight. On some keys, especially for drill presses, the pin on the end is spring-loaded so it pops out of the chuck on release. This prevents the tool being activated when the key is in place.

Some drills have keyless chucks, and the tightening is done instead by hand pressure. This makes the operation quicker, and avoids the necessity of keeping track of a key. It is possible to replace a keyed chuck with a keyless chuck, or even to replace a chuck if it becomes damaged.

Hand drill

Materials: **Wood**
Metal
Plastic
Drywall
Kits: **Craft**
Child's
Price: **$**
Necessity: **oooo**
Skill level: **o**

The *hand drill* is used much less commonly since the electric drill was introduced, but they are still very useful for drilling small holes or when an electric or cordless drill is too cumbersome. Their simplicity and relatively slow speed make them a safe tool to use.

The hand drill is operated like a hand-cranked eggbeater. One hand holds the handle on the top and the other turns the crank on the side. The gearing makes the bit spin several times faster than the crank is turned.

Hand drills are still sold new, though good-quality used or antique ones can often be found inexpensively at garage sales and flea markets. If you buy a used one, be sure all of the pieces are there and in good condition. Make sure the gears mesh well and the crank wheel isn't chewed up or wobbly. There are variations you might run across.

Variations:
Breast plate drill is a large, heavy-duty hand drill. It has a curved plate on the end, allowing the operator to press down on the drill with the chest. They bore large holes through tough material. They are more of a curiosity than a practical tool.
Variable direction ratchet. If you are left-handed, you may find a hand drill rather awkward to use, as the handle will crank toward you rather than away. A ratchet mechanism allows the crank to operate in either direction and spin the bit in the direction in which it cuts. They are rare, but they are out there!

Brace and auger

Materials: **Wood**
Price: **$$**
Necessity: **OO**
Skill level: **OO**

The *brace and auger* is used to drill accurate, flat-bottomed holes in wood. The brace is a crank-shaped device with a chuck at one end and a free-spinning handle on the other. The auger bit cuts the hole. The augers are interchangeable, with different sizes available for different hole diameters, from ¼ to 1 inch.

At the auger's tip is a small, threaded point that centers it and corkscrews the bit down into the wood. Spiral flutes run up the auger's length, carrying wood chips out of the hole. On the top end is a square shaft grabbed by the brace's chuck. Turning the crank-shaped brace slowly turns the auger, to drill the hole.

Most braces have a mechanism to lock the chuck in place or allow it to ratchet in one direction or the other, which helps when working in a tight space.

Versions of this tool have existed for thousands of years, and one has been documented in use around 100 CE, in China, but was not commonly found in Europe until the fifteenth century. Today the brace is overlooked in favor of the electric drill fitted with a twist bit or, for larger holes, a spade bit. But the brace and auger does have the advantage in that the auger bits are long, compared to other bits, allowing the drilling of very deep holes. A sharp auger will perform well on large-diameter holes, without the need to resort to a Forstner bit and a drill press (see pages 95 and 104 respectively). Also, because the tool is slow and hand-powered, it allows for stopping quickly if something unexpected happens, an especially useful feature when drilling through walls or floors.

New braces and auger sets can be expensive, but they often turn up at garage sales or flea markets.

Push drill

Materials: **Wood**
Metal
Price: **$**
Necessity: **OO**
Skill level: **O**

A *push drill* is used to make small-diameter holes in wood and soft metals. It is a supplementary tool in any tool collection, or a compact alternative to the cordless drill, yet no longer in common use. Also known as a *Yankee drill*, it has a spring-loaded handle that is pushed down over a shaft with double spiral-shaped grooves milled into its surface. At the bottom end of the shaft is a small chuck that can hold one of its drill or screwdriver bits stored in its handle.

When the handle is pushed down, pins inside ride in the spiral grooves in the shaft. This turns the shaft, with the drill bit attached to the end of it. An internal spring returns the handle to its starting position at the end of the shaft.

At one time, carpenters who installed door hardware furniture favored push drills. It enabled them to quickly drill holes and drive screws for door hinges, much like cordless electric drills do today. While the push drill does not have the versatility of the cordless drill, it is less expensive and more compact, making it ideal for attaching door hinges.

Corded electric drill

Materials: **Wood**
Metal
Plastic
Drywall
Masonry
Kits: **Home**
Price: **$$–$$$**
Necessity: **OOOO**
Skill level: **O**

Shaped and held like an overweight pistol, the *electric drill* is a brawny, reliable instrument. It can make holes of differing sizes in a wide range of materials. It has the power to spin hole saws and spade bits to make large holes, and will accommodate masonry bits for drilling into concrete and brick.

A trigger activates the motor, and determines how fast the bit spins, giving great control of the tool. Also within reach of the same trigger finger is a switch allowing a change of spin direction of the bit. This is handy for removing screws or dislodging a stuck bit.

Electric drills are available with ⅜- and ½-inch chucks, that may be keyed or keyless. This chuck dimension denotes the maximum size of bit which can be inserted into the drill. Drills with ½-inch chucks are more powerful.

There are specialized grades or variations of the tool.

Variations:
Hammer drills are handheld electric drills used to drill into masonry. The bit not only spins, but oscillates up and down slightly. This hammering action allows the bit to cut through more effectively.

Screw guns are designed specifically for instaling drywall with screws. At a glance it looks like an ordinary electric drill, but with a hollow nose cone and a screwdriver bit near its tip. The bit engages the screw head and drives it into the wall until it is in so far the bit looses its grip. In the process the nose cone dimples the sheet rock surface. Accessory screw tips mimicking this action are available for use in both corded and cordless electric drills.

Cordless electric drill

Materials: **Wood**
Metal
Plastic
Masonry
Kits: **Apartment**
Home
Price: **$$$**
Necessity: ⬡⬡⬡⬡
Skill level: ⬡

A *cordless electric drill* can handle most light- to medium-duty drilling and screw-driving operations. They are ideal for simple, quick jobs and avoid the need for outlets and extension cords—and of course, they are portable.

Like corded electric drills, cordless drills have a trigger switch mounted on the handle to activate and vary the speed of the motor, and a switch to reverse its direction. Most have keyless chucks (see page 97).

They also have two features that corded drills do not. The first is a two-speed "transmission" that lets the chuck turn at a low speed with a lot of torque for drilling large holes, or with less torque but high speeds for drilling small holes or driving screws. A lever on top of the drill "shifts" the gears. The second feature is a variable clutch which allows the motor to disengage when it encounters resistance preventing over-tightening or damage to screws. Turning a collar located behind

the chuck sets the amount of resistance required to cause the motor to disengage.

Consider using a mid-range cordless drill for everyday use and a regular electric drill for heavier jobs. Unless the cordless drill you select is one of the beefier models, it may not have the torque to drill large (1¼-inch or more) holes, or may drain the battery quickly in the process.

Two types of battery systems are commonly in use: Ni-MH (nickel metal hydride) and Ni-Cd (nickel cadmium). Ni-MH is the environmentally sound choice, although it tends to have a shorter life span. Batteries also have different power ratings: 7.2, 9.6, 12, 14.4, and 18 volts are commonly available. (Each battery pack consists of a series of individual 1.2 volt cells wired together.) The higher the power the more expensive and heavier the drill, and the higher voltage batteries generally have a shorter life span as a result of the heat they generate. A moderately priced 12-volt drill will serve

well for most tasks. If you intend to bore large holes frequently, then an 18-volt drill is a better option.

Batteries and chargers are not inter-changeable between manufacturers, so it is worth researching if you plan to buy other cordless tools such as jigsaws or circular saws, as you will not want to deal with incompatible pieces from different producers or have a different charger for each of them.

It's also a good idea to handle different drills before you buy, to check whether you are comfortable with the balance or grip, or find a particular trigger or direction switch more or less awkward to use. Narrow your selection down to the type of performance you need, and choose the one that feels best for you.

There are many accessories you can buy for a drill, and the combination screw bit/countersink bit is the most useful. One end pre-drills and countersinks a hole for a screw. The other end has a Phillips bit to drive the screw. It eliminates constantly changing bits or needing two drills to hand. It also saves a lot of time on do-it-yourself projects (see page 94).

TOP TOOL TIP

A carpenter's myth holds that a battery should be drawn down completely before recharging. In fact, you should never fully discharge a battery, as it damages the cells. If performance becomes noticeably lacking, recharge as soon as possible. Every ten or 12 times you recharge a battery, fully charge it for 24 to 48 hours.

For best results, store and charge a battery at room temperature. Let a warm, recently depleted battery cool before you charge it. A battery that is too hot or too cold will not charge or operate at peak efficiency.

Also, when a battery no longer holds its charge, dispose of it responsibly, at a recycling center.

Drill press

Materials: **Wood**
Metal
Plastic
Price: **$$$$**
Necessity: **OOO**
Skill level: **OO**

A *drill press* is a staple piece of equipment of woodworking and metalworking shops, whether bench-mounted or free-standing. It drills perfectly vertical holes in almost any dense, solid material.

Operation is simple. The work piece sits on a table and a drill bit is plunged down into it when a lever on the side of the machine is pulled. The tool is built around a vertical post attached to a heavy cast-steel base plate. A table to support the work piece is mounted to the post so that it can be pivoted, raised and lowered. Most presses have a crank attached to a rack-and-pinion system to assist with these adjustments.

Attached to the top of the post is the "head," which contains the moving parts. At the rear is the motor. At the front is the quill, and inside the quill is the spindle which the chuck is attached. A drive belt connects pulleys on the spindle to pulleys on the motor, which turns the spindle, the chuck and the drill bit. Different operating speeds can be obtained by placing the belt over different combinations of pulleys.

A depth stop adjustment ensures a hole is no deeper than required and allows for a series of holes to be set to identical depth. By attaching a fence to the table to slide the work along, a series of holes can be drilled in a perfectly straight line.

The press's power and stability allows holes to be drilled using wide bits such as Forstner or extra large twist bits (see page 95). The strength of the motor and amount of vertical travel in the quill determines the maximum size of the holes, while the size of the drill press is determined by the amount of depth measured horizontally from the center of the drill bit to the center of the support post.

Small drill stands are available onto which a standard, handheld electric drill can be mounted to mimic the functions of a drill press, but a small bench-top drill press is a much better option.

Hollow bit mortiser

Materials: **Wood**
Price: **$$$$**
Necessity: **OO**
Skill level: **OOO**

The *hollow bit mortiser* is the only tool that will drill a square hole. Woodworkers use it for mortise and tenon joinery, where a rectangular tab (tenon) is cut on the end of one piece, to fit into a rectangular pocket (mortise) in another piece.

The hollow bit mortiser is motorized, combining the work of both a drill and a chisel. The cutting piece is a square, hardened-steel tube with a sharp, chisel edge ground onto four sides of one end. A drill bit is centered inside.

There are two versions of the tool: a stand-alone machine; or an accessory to a drill press. In both configurations, a lever mechanism plunges the mortising tool down into the work piece, which is held in place on a table below. As the tool advances into the wood, the spinning drill bit clears the waste from the middle of the hole and the sharp edges of the square tube pare away at the walls. A series of drilled squares, side by side, makes the rectangular mortise. The tool has a stop mechanism to prevent drilling too deep and keeps each pass consistent.

This is a very specialized tool, and if your projects regularly require mortises, it is a real timesaver.

Plug cutter

Materials: **Wood**
Price: **$**
Necessity: **OOOO**
Skill level: **O**

Screws can be easily concealed in a piece of wood by countersinking their heads below the surface and gluing wood plugs on top of them. The function of the plug is to disguise the presence of the screw head for aesthetic, or in the case of boatbuilding, for protective reasons.

Plugs are available commercially, but with a *plug cutter* they are easy to make yourself, using scrap wood left over from a project. Homemade plugs will match the grain and color of the wood in a project, to make them almost invisible—or, can be made in a contrasting wood.

Different cutter sizes are available for different sized holes.

The plug cutter functions like a tiny hole saw (see page 96). It is placed in a drill press or held very straight in an electric drill and advanced into the surface of the wood. The cutting edges make a ring-shaped groove in the wood, leaving a tapered wood "island" in the center. A hole of the same size as the plug cutter is drilled deep in the positions where the screws are to be inserted.

There is a lot of friction in this type of cut and a risk of overheating the bit, which will make it dull faster. If making a lot of plugs, stop to allow the bit to cool occasionally. After drilling as many plugs as required, the plugs are split away from the board by putting a slotted screwdriver into the groove and twisting it, which will pop the plug out.

The plugs are tapered so that when glued and tapped into the plug hole above the screw head, they wedge into place, making a tight joint around the edge. Ensure that the surface grain of the top of the plug lines up with the grain of the surface being plugged. Any excess can be pared away with a chisel and then sanded flush with the surrounding wood.

The plug cutter is a simple and inexpensive tool that can add a finished look to woodwork while still allowing the use of simple, screwed connections.

Rotating head punch

Materials: **Leather**
Rubber
Cork
Vinyl
Kits: **Craft**
Price: **$**
Necessity: **O**
Skill level: **OOO**

A *punch* is basically a steel tube with a sharp cutting edge ground on one end, working much like a round chisel. Tapping the punch with a hammer drives the cutting edge through most soft materials, cutting a neat, round hole. This simple punch is sold in craft stores and in automotive supply stores, and is also known as a gasket punch.

The *rotating head punch* is a combination of six punches in one. It is held like a pair of pliers and the work piece is placed between the jaws. On the lower jaw is a small anvil. On the upper jaw is a rotating head with various-sized hole punches. Dial up the selected hole size and place it to strike the anvil when the handle is squeezed.

Place a piece of leather on the anvil under the material being punchd to prevent damage to the cutting edge.

A punch is especially useful around the holidays, when you discover your belt needs a few more holes for expansion!

Holding and supporting work

Without a sturdy base on which to work and a secure means to hold a piece of work, it is difficult to obtain the best results. To avoid frustration and for safety's sake, it is important to support a work piece during each step of fabrication, repair, or assembly.

General rules

- Think of your workbench as a tool and care for it as such. Do not drill or cut into the bench top. Use a replaceable cover to protect it when gluing, painting, or constructing other messy projects.

- If you do not have a designated work area or workshop, consider instead a folding or portable bench.

- Use a bench hook to hold small projects.

Beginner's class

Clamps are available for almost any size project. Below is a brief overview of the common types and a comparison of some of the clamps listed in this section:

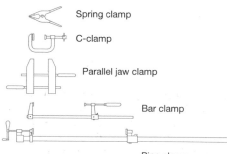

Spring clamp

C-clamp

Parallel jaw clamp

Bar clamp

Pipe clamp

Spring clamps (page 122): These work like large clothes pins. They don't exert much pressure, but can be applied and removed quickly using only one hand.

C-clamps (page 120): Many different size C-clamps are available, but those between 1 and 6 inches are most common. Their strong, rigid frames mean they can deliver a large amount of pressure to a small area.

Parallel jaw clamps (page 119): The broad surface area of ther jaws distributes pressure more evenly and that, combined with their wooden jaws, makes them less likely to dent or mar a wood work piece.

Bar clamps (page 118): These are used for clamping larger projects like drawers or

- Ensure the work piece will be adequately supported throughout the entire process.

- If you're having a difficult time holding the item you're working on, build a jig to hold the work in a way that allows you to proceed safely.

- Keep clamping surfaces clear and clean, as debris can damage the surface of a work piece.

- Place scraps of wood between the work and the jaws of a clamp or vise to distribute the pressure and to avoid scratching, denting, or discoloring the work piece.

- Assemble your project beforehand without the use of glue or fasteners, to ensure all the pieces fit properly. Use this opportunity to decide how many clamps you willl need and where they will be positioned.

- Arrange the clamps on the work piece to apply pressure evenly.

- Do not use a clamp or vise to force objects together. If they do not mate properly, find out why and correct the problem.

boxes. Their maximum capacity depends on the length of the bar. Clamps with bars from 6 to 36 inches long are available.

Pipe clamps (page 118): Pipe clamps are similar to bar clamps except that they can be made much longer, (up to several feet) since they use stiff steel pipe as the "bar." The clamping mechanism will also deliver more pressure than the smaller, lighter bar clamps. This makes pipe clamps suitable for very large projects such as furniture and cabinetry.

The illustration (right) shows other holding devices as they would be located on a workbench. A **bench hook** (page 116) for holding small pieces is shown hooked over the one edge of the bench. Holes for

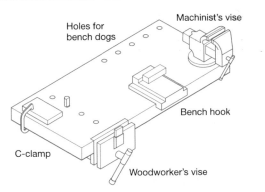

Machinist's vise

Holes for bench dogs

Bench hook

C-clamp

Woodworker's vise

bench dogs (page 113) are along two edges. A **woodworker's vise** is positioned at the left end, and a **machinist's vise** (page 114) for metal work is placed at the right end. If you have the space, two separate benches would be ideal; one for woodworking and another for metal work.

Saw horses

Materials: **Wood**
Metal
Plastic
Glass
Ceramic
Price: **$–$$**
Necessity: **OOOO**
Skill level: **O**

Saw horses are a fairly low-tech affair, and quite often can be made from scrap material when intended to last only the duration of a specific job. Alternatively, they can be purchased readymade, or as a ready-to-assemble kit. Their function is to support items up off the floor to be worked on. The best height, to place material at a comfortable position for sawing, is about 2 feet.

Folding saw horses made of plastic or sheet metal can be purchased at many home centers. They are also available with metal or plastic bracket attachments into which can be inserted pieces of 2 x 4 to make a quick set of horses that are equally easily disassembled. This gives flexibility in deciding on the height required. Tall saw horses make painting and finish work more comfortable, while short horses are useful for positioning large case goods at a convenient height for work.

Besides supporting material during sawing, plywood can be stacked on them; they can hold a platform to form a small scaffold; trim can be laid out on them for painting; they will support cabinets during assembly, work counters to be cut or, with an extra sheet of plywood, they'll even form a table top for the lunch banquet.

Portable workbench

Materials:	**Wood**
	Metal
	Plastic
	Glass
	Ceramic
Kits:	**Home**
Price:	**$$**
Necessity:	**OOOO**
Skill level:	**O**

A folding, portable workbench designed and manufactured by Black & Decker, and named the *Workmate*™, is an ingenious compromise between a dedicated workbench and working at the kitchen table. Since it folds relatively flat, it is well suited for use as a temporary workstation, and when not in use, it can be collapsed and stored in a closet, corner or even under a bed.

The top is divided into either two or three sections depending on the model. The outer sections are connected with a pair of cranks and threaded rods that allow them to be moved together or apart to clamp a work piece in place. Turning both cranks at the same time moves the sections in parallel. Turning one or the other will open or draw together one end alone, enabling odd-shaped items to be clamped securely. Triangular grooves are cut in the meeting faces of the sections in order to clamp tubes or pipe. Holes in the top accept plastic plugs, which function as

bench dogs to hold a work piece or grab the edges of a large flat item to clamp.

It can be set at two different working heights—leaving the legs folded puts the work surface at a good height for use as a saw horse, while extending the legs brings it up to a more comfortable bench height to serve as a base for small power tools, such as a miter saw or benchtop planer.

Several models are available. The brawniest has a decent-sized work surface and will support up to 550 lbs, yet is still light enough to fold up and carry away.

Workbench

Materials: **Wood**
Metal
Plastic
Glass
Ceramic
Price: **$$–$$$$**
Necessity: **OOOO**
Skill level: **O**

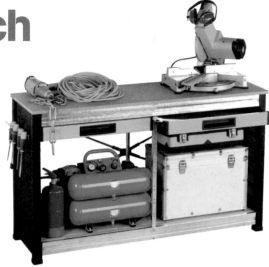

Traditional woodworking benches are for holding materials during sawing, planing, and joinery work. The Romans built some of the first workbenches. These were simply large, heavy, wooden tables with a wood strip pegged to the end. The wood strip and table-top prevented the piece from falling or sliding. Two thousand years later, the *workbench* still does basically that same job. It positions the work piece so that it can be comfortably, safely, and efficiently worked, and it holds the piece securely so all effort is applied to shaping, instead of it moving around. This makes the whole process safer, and allows for better concentration on the work.

The construction of the bench and the design of the devices attached to it have evolved. The bench top once consisted of large slabs of wood, but today's tops are made from strips of laminated hardwood. They are smooth and flat, which helps ensure the pieces made are assembled true and square.

A bench top is not much use without a base to support it off the floor. On many, a simple trestle-style frame is used to provide a heavy, rigid base that remains light enough to move. In a small shop, it is worth building storage shelves or cabinets into the base of the bench to make the most of the space. This also adds weight to the workbench, making it steadier.

Vises, *bench dogs*, and *clamps* are the most basic items to use to fasten a work piece to the workbench. Pre-made screw-on or clamp-on vises (see pages 114, 118, 120) can be installed on most benches. Some more expensive versions have vises built into the bench top, allowing a corner or an end of the bench to open up and form a slot in which to hold material. Built-in vises also have holes in their large wood jaws to accommodate bench dogs.

Bench dogs

Materials: **Workbench**
Price: **$**
Necessity: **OOO**
Skill level: **O**

Bench dogs are round or rectangular pins made from wood or metal with a springy tab attached to one side. The dogs fit snugly into holes cut into the bench top and are inserted so that a small part pokes out above the work surface. This provides a stop for the work piece to rest against. A row of holes down the length of each side of the bench allows the repositioning of the dogs for different size projects. On an inexpensive bench, screwing a stop block into the top will have the same effect, but without the adjustment.

When a dog is built into a vise and another dog is set in the bench top, the vise can be closed and the work piece squeezed between the two, to hold it securely in place.

Vise

Materials: Wood
Metal
Plastic
Glass
Ceramic
Kits: Machine and metal work
Price: $–$$$
Necessity: ⬡⬡⬡⬡
Skill level: ⬡

Vises are made to hold a work piece firmly in place on a workbench. As long as the work cannot move in the vise, then the entire weight of the bench is available to resist the forces applied to the piece as it is cut and shaped.

Traditional-style woodworking benches have vises built into them, but more often clamp-on or bolt-on vises are added to a simple bench top. There are specialized types of vises, and the *bench vise* and the *face vise* are the two most common.

The bench vise, or *machinist's vise*, mounts on top of the bench surface. It is used to hold metal and pipe to be cut, bent, shaped, or filed. Light- to medium-duty versions can be clamped to the edge of the bench and also be quickly removed. Heavy-duty versions have a base screwed into the bench top. The vise is made from cast steel and has one fixed jaw and one movable jaw. Turning a bar handle on the end of the movable jaw turns a long screw inside the vise, drawing the two jaws

together. Surrounding the screw is a steel channel protecting the screw from damage and debris, and keeping the jaws aligned.

Well-made vises have removable etched metal pads where the jaws touch so they can be replaced if damaged, or if a softer, non-marring surface is needed. On larger vises, a secondary pair of curved, toothed jaws for holding round stock is found inside the throat of the main jaws. Most heavy-duty models have a swivel base to pivot the vise and lock it into whichever position works best for a given process.

The fixed jaw of the bench vise is beefy enough to serve as a base on which to hammer and shape material. Some vises have an anvil cast into the main body of the vise to provide a surface for heavy pounding and shaping.

The face vise, or *woodworker's vise*, has a pair of wide, flat jaws connected by a large central screw. A guide bar on either side of the screw helps keep the jaws parallel. Unlike the bench vise, the face

vise is almost nothing but jaws. It clamps bigger pieces and applies pressure evenly over a broad area. Applying too much pressure to a small area can easily twist the vise and damage it.

A face vise should be positioned near a corner of the workbench so the top of the jaws are flush with the work surface. Holes in the jaws allow sacrificial wood pads to be screwed to the jaws—to avoid marring the work piece. The jaws and pads should be kept clean of glue and debris.

The best-quality vises feature large jaws and heavy castings. They may include a quick-release feature for the screw, which disengages the threads so the jaws slide closed quickly, rather than having to continually spin the handle. A retractable "dog" mounted into the movable jaw is another desirable feature.

Bench hook

Materials:	**Wood**
	Metal
Kits:	**Craft**
Price:	**$**
Necessity:	**⬡⬡⬡⬡**
Skill level:	**⬡**

1   2

Craftsmen have been making their own *bench hooks* for centuries. They are not available to buy: you will have to make it yourself as a simple project using scraps or leftover materials.

The bench hook consists of two rectangular pieces of wood or plywood about 1 foot long.

The cleat on top of the bench hook acts as a stop against which to hold small items while working on them with a plane, chisel, saw, or other tool. The cleat on the bottom hooks over the edge of the workbench (*see figure 1*). Once a work piece is held securely, careful, measured movements with the tool keep the process safe and more accurate because the piece does not slide around (*see figure 2*). It is easy to reposition it quickly to work at a different angle, and the hook helps protect the work surface from stray cuts. The extra wide piece on the bottom prevents a saw from accidentally hitting the bench top on completion of a cut.

TOP TOOL TIP:
Here's how to make an 8-inch wide, and a 10-inch wide bench hook:

- Cut two strips of wood, one 8 inches wide, one 10 inches wide.
- Glue and screw the pieces together.
- Install the screws from the bottom.

Bench hooks are useful for many small jobs—not just woodworking projects—and are a good way to protect a table when working elsewhere than at a dedicated workbench.

Jigs and fixtures

Materials: **Wood**
Metal
Plastic
Glass
Ceramic
Price: **$–$$$**
Necessity: **OOO**
Skill level: **OOO**

Jigs and *fixtures* are more of a category of items than tools in their own right. Jigs are accessories added to or used in conjunction with other tools. They can broaden a tool's capabilities or make a process safer, more consistent, or more efficient, and are either manufactured or can be homemade, are simple or complex, but they are usually specialized and tailored to a specific task.

One of the most common jigs is the miter box (see page 76), which holds a handsaw at a number of different angles for an accurate cut. It is an example of a jig that is used to guide a tool. Other jigs are designed to *hold* the work piece securely. A *V-block* is one of the simplest. It is a block with a V-shaped groove cut into it. A round bar, or dowel, will sit in the groove and not roll around during drilling or when being sawn.

A more complex jig is the *tenoning jig* which is used to hold a work piece vertically as it is passed over the blade of a table saw to cut the "cheeks" off the sides of the tenon. This allows a table saw to safely make a cut that would otherwise be too dangerous.

There are books available dedicated entirely to jigs, some applicable to just one tool, such as the table saw or the router. Others are more general in scope.

Bar and pipe clamps

Materials: **Wood**
Metal
Plastic
Glass
Ceramic
Price: **$**
Necessity: **OOOO**
Skill level: **O**

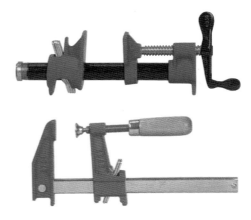

Bar clamps have two jaws, which are attached to a steel bar. One of these jaws holds a threaded rod with a handle on one end and a pivoting foot on the other. While one jaw is fixed in place, the other is free to slide up and down the bar in order to accommodate work of different sizes. As the handle is turned to tighten the clamp, the sliding jaw twists a little and jams in place on the bar, making a rigid, C-shaped frame. The sliding jaws on good-quality clamps have a stack of "clutch" plates built into them to help to lock the jaw in place.

Bar clamps for general use range in size from 6 to 24 inches long, and tiny versions are available for small jobs, such as instrument- or model-making. Giant bar clamps also are available but *pipe clamps* have become the more commonly used alternative.

The jaws of a pipe clamp are designed to fit on a length of ¾ inch- or 1 inch-diameter steel water pipe rather than on

a rectangular bar. The fixed jaw screws onto one end of the pipe and the moveable jaw is free to slide along its length. The jaws are sold as a set and the pipe is bought separately.

Another version of the bar clamp has a steel and plastic trigger-action. The movable jaw has a pistol-grip handle with a broad trigger that allows you to hold and quickly close the clamp with only one hand. The jaws also reverse on the bar so when the trigger is squeezed, the jaws are forced apart.

Bar clamps are often used two at a time to apply even pressure across a work piece, so it is usually wise to buy them in pairs, sized 18-inches. Rubber covers are useful to slip onto the tips of the jaws, to avoid marring a work piece.

Hand screw

Materials: **Wood**
Metal
Plastic
Glass
Ceramic
Price: **$**
Necessity: **OOOO**
Skill level: **O**

1

Hand screws, also known as *parallel jaw clamps*, are used in woodworking to hold parts in place during fabrication and assembly.

Early parallel jaw clamps consisted of a pair of wood screws threaded through a pair of hardwood jaws. Tightening or loosening the screws allowed the jaws to move parallel to each other. Each screw had to be turned an equal amount, or else the threads could bind.

The screws in modern clamps engage small round metal inserts. Instead of forcing the screws to run straight through the jaws, the inserts pivot. This means the screws no longer have to be tightened the same amount, allowing the clamping of odd-shaped objects. The pressure of the jaws can be varied and applied at different points by tightening one screw more than the other.

The downside of this flexibility is the jaws have to be set parallel with each other again when clamping something flat.

The easiest way to do this is to first close the jaws all the way so that they touch all along their length, then open them back up to the size required. To keep the jaws parallel, ensure both screws are turned the same amount. Hold a screw handle in each hand. Then rotate as if cranking bicycle pedals. Crank one way to open the clamp, crank the other to close (*see figure 1*).

Hand screws are available with jaws ranging from 4 to 20 inches long, though 6 to 12 inches are most common. If you need a special sized or shaped jaw, kits are available containing the screws, handles, and threaded inserts to enable you to custom-make your own clamps.

C-clamp

Materials: **Wood**
Metal
Plastic
Glass
Ceramic
Price: **$**
Necessity: **OOOO**
Skill level: **O**

1

C-clamps work well for small clamping jobs, or where a large amount of pressure is required.

There are four parts to a C-clamp. The main piece is the C-shaped frame, which is made from aluminum or cast steel, though cheaper versions are made from stamped steel. They are named C-clamps because of their shape, but are also known as *G-clamps* because the entire assembly, which includes a threaded rod screwed through one side of the frame, resembles the letter G. On the end of the rod in the mouth of the frame is a pivoting foot that makes clamping odd-shaped objects easier. On the other end is a sliding handle called a *tommy bar*. Turning the rod closes the clamp mouth.

The maximum gap between the foot and the opposite side of the frame determines the size of the clamp, which can range from 1 to 10 inches or more, although the 1- to 6-inch clamps are the most common. The clamp's throat determines how far in from the edge an item can be held.

The C-clamp is useful because the rigid frame does not flex like a bar clamp. However, avoid over-tightening the clamp as overstressing can damage it.

TOP TOOL TIP
To quickly close or open the clamp, hold the threaded rod in one hand and spin the frame around like a party noisemaker (*see figure 1*).

Spring clamp

Materials: **Wood**
Metal
Plastic
Glass
Ceramic
Price: **$**
Necessity: **OOOO**
Skill level: **O**

Spring clamps work like giant clothes pins, but instead of wooden jaws, the spring clamp has large plastic or stamped metal pieces, often with a rubber covering on the grips and tips of the jaws. They are connected by a coil spring in the middle to keep the jaws closed.

Spring clamps are best suited for small or lightweight projects requiring little pressure, and are good for temporarily holding a pattern or work piece. They take up little space and can be utilised with just one hand. However, they do have a limited capacity and large pieces can easily be knocked out of alignment because of the light pressure the spring clamp provides. Very small metal spring clamps are available, but for small craft projects or model-making, it is often easier to use domestic clothes pins.

Spring clamps are also useful to clip a tarp, drop cloth in place, or hold the end of a tape measure in an awkward spot.

Strap clamp

Materials: **Wood**
Metal
Plastic
Glass
Ceramic
Price: **$**
Necessity: **OOOO**
Skill level: **O**

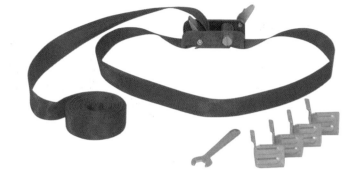

A *strap clamp* works much like a belt that holds up your pants. You wrap the clamp around an object and use a ratcheting and buckle mechanism to draw the strap tight, and apply even pressure around the perimeter of the work piece.

It is particularly useful during any final assembly and glue-up of closed items, such as picture frames and boxes, especially those with mitered corners. One or two strap clamps can do the work of a half dozen or more bar clamps.

The clamp consists of a strip of nylon webbing several feet long, with one end attached to a spool that is held in a stamped metal frame. One end of the spool is hexagon-shaped, and a wrench is used to turn it and wind up the strap. On the other end of the spool is a ratchet which prevents the strap from unwinding until the release lever is pulled. The free end of the strap is woven through a pair of slots in the metal frame, which makes the strap into a closed loop. When clamping

an object, put it inside the loop and pull on the loose end of the strap to draw it down snug. Use a wrench to wind the strap, drawing it tight.

When selecting a strap clamp, ensure the ratchet and release operate smoothly.

Plastic L-shaped corner blocks are available to help keep corners square and protect them from the webbing. These are placed between the strap and the corners of the work piece to focus pressure at these points.

Miter clamp

Materials: **Wood**
Metal
Plastic
Glass
Ceramic
Price: **$**
Necessity: **OOOO**
Skill level: **O**

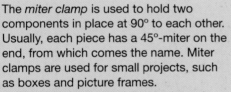

The *miter clamp* is used to hold two components in place at 90° to each other. Usually, each piece has a 45°-miter on the end, from which comes the name. Miter clamps are used for small projects, such as boxes and picture frames.

The clamp consists of an L-shaped cast-metal frame. The inside edges turn up to form a pair of fences, 90° to each other. Opposite each of these is a foot on the end of a threaded rod. By tightening these, a work piece is clamped between the foot and the fence.

Some clamps have a built-in saw guide so they can be used as a makeshift miter box, but cutting on a more substantial tool gives better results. Once the pieces are prepared, each is placed in the clamp. Each piece needs to be adjusted back and forth to make sure the corner is properly aligned, before the clamp is drawn down.

Several manufacturers of trigger-grip bar clamps offer accessory L-shaped jaws for their tools to slip over existing ones.

When the clamp closes, these nest together, holding the work piece at a right-angle. Other heavier-duty clamps use this nesting principle and have a pair of jaws closed with a single hand screw.

In addition, there are L-shaped blocks of metal or plastic available to clamp in place on the inside of a corner to hold two items at 90°. These can be used with standard bar clamps and are a good option for larger-scale projects. Strap clamps and homemade clamping jigs can also deliver good results.

Shaping

Shaping work can range from simply rounding off a sharp edge on a flat sheet of material, right through to the intricate carving of a headboard. When building something from scratch, preliminary work often needs to be done to prepare the stock for layout and cutting. When that is done and the parts are rough cut to size, the next step is to shape the parts to their final form. Whether you are building a piece of furniture or filing to fit during a repair, the basic rules apply.

General rules

- Powered shaping tools have blades that are either discarded when dull or need to be professionally sharpened. Small hand tools, such as chisels and planes, can be sharpened using a grinder and sharpening stone (see pages 145 and 210).

- A lot of shaping work is done with hand-guided tools, so thinking ahead is essential to appreciate where and what the tool will do should it slip during operation. Keep items that will damage the tool, such as clamps and bench dogs, out of the way.

Beginner's class

When planing, carving or chiseling wood, you should work with the grain for best results. But what does that really mean?

1 Plastics and metals have a homogenous composition. Like a block of cheese, they behave much the same no matter which direction you cut or work them. Wood is different as it is composed of individual fibers that are bound together. These fibers are the plant's tubes that once carried nutrients through the trunk of the tree. They are parallel for the most part, but not perfectly so. The tree tapers as you go further up, and the fibers curve around branches, wounds or other obstructions.

2 When a tree trunk is cut up into boards, it is sawn lengthwise. As a result, the wood fibers (or grain) are roughly parallel to the long edge of the boards. If you look at the short end, you'll see alternating light and dark bands, which are the tree's growth rings. You can follow these bands around onto the face of the board and see how they run up the board's length. As you follow them up the board, you'll see they aren't truly parallel to the edges of the board and that some trail away and run "off the edge" due to curves in the grain or because of how the board was cut.

- Using tools designed for wood to shape metal will do damage. Using fine-toothed files intended for work on metal to shape and smooth wood will make the job really hard work, and slow.

- Gain a sense for how the material behaves as you work with it. Practice on some scrap. With wood, for instance, plane or slice with the grain to prevent digging in or tearing up the surface.

- Use tools that take large, coarse bites from material when beginning and move toward finer, more precise tools once the basic form is roughed out. Sometimes it may be more efficient to use a saw to cut away large pieces of excess material.

- When trying to fit something trim close to the cut line, but not right on it, then do a trial fit. Continue paring away and test-fitting until you achieve the fit.

- To make multiple copies of an item, use a template, form or jig to duplicate the shape.

- When preparing rough stock, first flatten one face, then make the other parallel to it. Next, one edge is made straight and square to the faces. Finally, the opposite edge is cut parallel to the first.

- Avoid allowing waste to accumulate. Shavings, dust, and metal filings can clog tools, make the floor slippery, and could dangerously clutter the work area.

3 Working with wood is like petting a cat. If you move your hand in the direction the fur wants to lay down, it will glide smoothly. If you stroke toward the ends of the fur, you ruffle it. Running an edge tool like a plane or chisel across a piece of wood works the same way. When the tool rides on the grain that is running off the edge the cutter shears off material cleanly. However, if you push the blade toward the exposed ends of the grain, it can dig in and

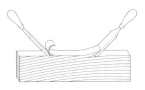

get stuck, and may split off a large piece rather than paring off a small amount, or may leave a rough splintered surface behind. This splintering action is called "tearout."

4 Be aware that grain, in a piece of wood, can change direction several times over the length of a board, which can make it difficult to work. This is why lumber is divided into different grades and price levels based on how straight and knot free (or clear) the grain is. Whichever grade you buy, it pays to select your lumber carefully and choose boards with the straightest, clearest grain and free of any warping or twisting.

Wood chisels

Materials: **Wood**
Price: **$–$$**
Necessity: OOOO
Skill level: OO

Chisels, or *flat-backed chisels* are used to shape wood. The tip of a chisel is ground at a bevel to form a sharp cutting edge which functions as a short, stout knife blade, severing the wood fibers as manual pressure is applied. A chisel can be used bevel-side up or down depending on the type of cut.

Some chisels are designed to withstand heavy blows from a wooden mallet to drive the blade through the wood, while others are used with hand pressure alone to slice away small shavings. Chisels are sold in sets of four and usually include ¼, ½, ¾, and 1-inch widths. These, as well as other sizes, can also be purchased individually.

The toughest, most basic chisel is the *butt chisel*. It has a short, stubby blade, often with a protective metal cap molded into the end. As a general rule, a wood chisel should not be struck with a metal hammer but the sturdy butt chisel is the exception to this. It will withstand some of the abuse required for fairly rough

carpentry work, yet it can also be used for finer tasks, such as mortising hinges into a doorframe.

Firmer chisels have thick blades with straight sides and are used for fine work that requires the strength of a mallet blow. A subset of firmer chisels are known as *mortising chisels,* which are thicker than they are wide, and are used for heavy cross-grain chopping when cutting a mortise. Both have a socket-style handle with a tapered tip that fits into a cone-shaped recess (socket) cast into the end of the blade. When struck with a mallet, the force of the blow helps to wedge the handle tighter into the socket.

Paring chisels are for lighter-duty work and are pushed by hand. They are used to pare away thin slices of wood. When doing this, one hand pushes the tool while the other guides the tip. Their blades are thinner than those of firmer chisels and the sides are beveled inward allowing the tool to fit into tight, acute corners.

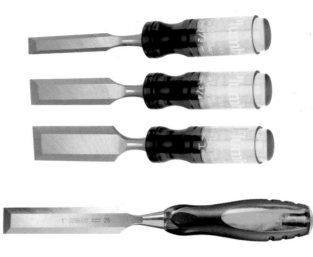

The handles of paring chisels are attached by using a tang, which is a long, thin extension of the blade that runs up into the handle through a hole in its center. The handle slides over the tang until it bears on a wide part of the chisel's neck called the bolster. A brass band called a ferrule is wrapped around the base of the handle to hold it in place and keep it from splitting apart.

Chisel handles are traditionally made from wood but are now more likely to be made from plastic or polypropylene. This, of course, does not have the same feel as wood, and the appearance certainly does not improve with age as wooden handles do, but they can be more durable and are more securely attached to the tool.

A sharp chisel is a pleasure to use, but a dull one is frustrating and dangerous. It's important to take good care of your chisels. Keep them sharp and always avoid dropping or banging them together, which will damage the edges. Most are

sold with protective plastic caps that slip over the cutting edge and it's a good idea to get into the habit of replacing these when work is finished. See page 210 for a description of the abrasive stones used to sharpen wood chisels.

Gouge

Materials: **Wood**
Price: **$–$$**
Necessity: **OOO**
Skill level: **OO**

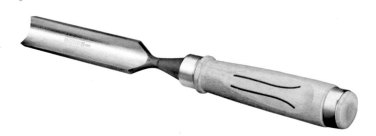

The wood chisels described previously (see page 126) are called flat-backed chisels because they have a flat, beveled cutting edge. However, chisels with a cutting edge that curves are known as *gouges*. A gouge will cut a U-shaped or V-shaped profile.

Just as with flat-backed chisels, there are *firmer gouges*, *paring gouges*, and *carving gouges*. They are available in a variety of shapes and with different degrees of curvature.

In addition, the edge is ground on the tool in two ways. Those with the bevel ground on the inside of the curve are called *in-cannel* gouges. These are used to chop and pare away the material in a straight line. *Out-cannel* gouges have the bevel ground on the outside of the curve and are used to carve away material to produce concave shapes.

Gouges are occasionally used in furniture-making, but their use is primarily to carve curved surfaces for anything from birds to carousel horses, and gouges are designed for many different types of work. They are sold individually, but purchasing a set is a simple way to acquire a range of basic profiles.

Drawknife

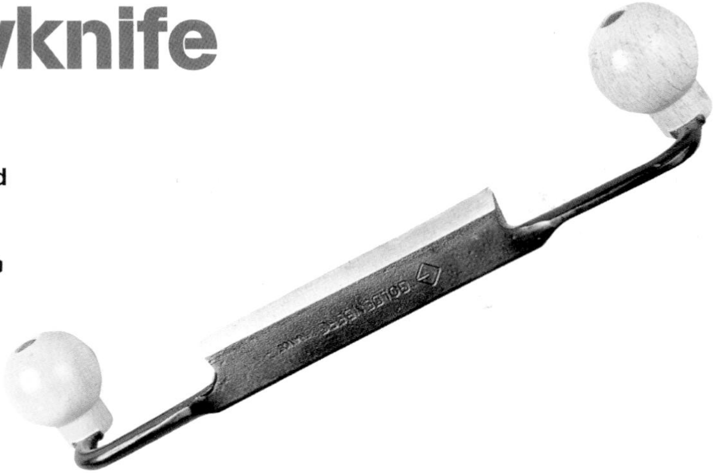

Materials: Wood
Price: $–$$
Necessity: OO
Skill level: OOO

A *drawknife* is used for shaping large pieces of wood in a similar way to a pocketknife, by carving or whittling away at a small stick. It comprises a very sharp, thick blade, 5 to 12 inches wide. The steel of the blade extends past each end of the cutting edge and bends at 90° or so, forming tangs that are covered by wooden handles. These handles are used to steer and control the blade as it is pulled through the wood. Broad, deep strokes quickly remove a lot of material for rough shaping and an experienced set of hands can pare away thin shavings for more precise cuts.

Many trades once used the drawknife, including shipbuilders and wheelwrights who used it to shape masts and spokes. It is much less used today, partly because it is a difficult tool to sharpen (a keen edge is very important), and partly because it requires practice and skill to use it well. Now a drawknife is used more usually to rough out shapes when carving or to round off material in preparation for turning on a lathe. Finer work is then done with a *spokeshave* (see page 138).

A relative of the drawknife is the *inshave*, which looks like a drawknife that has been bent into a U-shape. Inshaves are used to scoop out a hollow in a piece of wood, for example, to create the seat of a chair. Small inshaves, with a single handle, are called "scorps."

Files and rasps

Materials: **Wood**
Metal
Plastic
Kits: **Machine and metal work**
Home
Craft
Price: **$**
Necessity: **OOOO**
Skill level: **O**

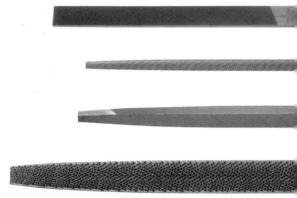

Files are bars of steel that are etched on their face and edges with hundreds of sharp, parallel serrations. They are used to shape and smooth a range of materials, from wood through to plastics.

Files have three basic applications of serration. *Curved cut* files have the serrations set in an arc down the face of the file, sometimes set onto the file's rounded or squared edges, and these are intended for use on soft metals.

Single cut files have their serrations set at an angle across the face of the file, and produce a smooth finish on the material being filed.

Double cut files have their serrations set in two opposing directions across the face, and this enables them to remove material more aggressively. An edge without any serration is called a "safe edge."

The larger the job with the more material to remove, the longer the file needs to be, while small files will provide a fine and smooth finish. Very small files, known as needle files, are used in model-making and jewelry work.

Files also have three levels of coarseness, common across the tool manufacturers, and measured by number of teeth per inch. The levels are named: A *bastard* file is the coarsest, at 26 teeth per inch (TPI). A *second cut* file has 36 TPI, and the finest, or *smooth* file has 60 TPI. There are also specific names for files with combinations of coarseness and serrations. A *mill* file, for example, is a long, rectangular, single cut, bastard file.

Different shapes suit different needs. Flat files are for general-purpose work, and there is a range of other shapes to fit a particular task, or work to be done in tight quarters. For really awkward spots, or when shaping a contoured cavity, files with curved and formed tips, called *rifflers*, are used.

Files are generally sold without handles, although handles can be made, or can be purchased separately. On one end of the

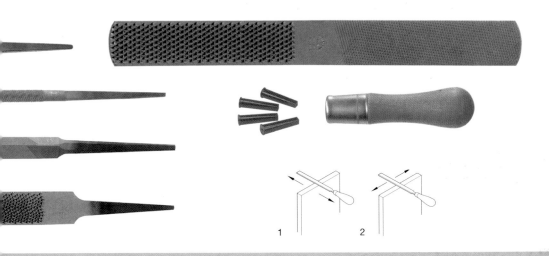

1   2

file is a tapered shank called a tang, over which a handle can fit. Never use a file without a handle in place, as the sharp tang can stab into the hand if it slips.

There are two techniques for the use of a file—cross filing and draw filing (*see figures 1 and 2*). Cross filing involves moving the file lengthwise across the work piece, which is the quickest way to remove material. Draw filing involves holding the file sideways with a hand on each end, moving down the work piece. This method provides a smooth finish and removes the marks that can be left by cross filing.

Rasps are similar tools to files, except that they have parallel rows of individually set teeth, rather than the continuous sets of serrations of files. Rasps are much coarser instruments and remove material more aggressively, and it is almost always necessary therefore to smooth the work with a file afterward. Because of the large abrasions they make, they are suitable only for wood or very soft metals.

A handy instrument to keep in a basic tool kit is a *four-in-hand rasp*, which combines two files and two rasps in one tool. One face is flat and the other curved. Each side is set with both file and rasp combination serrations.

To clean shavings from the file, a brush with stiff, short bristles called a file card will scour debris from the teeth.

Router

Materials: Wood
Plastic
Price: $$–$$$$
Necessity: OOO
Skill level: OO

Maneuvering a handheld tool that is spinning at 20,000 rpm may sound unappealing. But that describes the *router*, one of the most versatile power tools around. A range of tasks once requiring specialized tools and technique is now accomplished using a router, equipped with the right bit, guide, or jig.

Invented in 1905, the router is little more than an electric motor with a chuck-like fitting, known as a *collet*, that holds the shank of a cutting bit.

The motor is held by a base frame, which has two handles on its sides and a polycarbonate plate on the bottom. This plate rides on the surface of the work piece when the tool is in use. The depth and profile of a cut is determined by how high the bit sits relative to the base plate. Edge-cutting bits allow the tool to cut a shaped profile around the edge, either straight or curved, of the work piece. Grooving bits will cut a dado or a shaped slot through the middle of a work piece.

A grooving bit can also make complex or repetitive cuts around a template, or can cut perfect circles with the attachment of a pivoting arm. Both types of bits will have a round steel shank at their center, which can be ¼, ⅜ or ½ inches in diameter. One end of the shank is clamped into the collet. The other end has two high-speed steel wings the shape of the profile that the bit is to cut. A cutting edge is either ground on these wings directly or carbide cutting edges are brazed onto them.

Many edge-cutting bits have a pilot bearing feature not found on grooving bits. It is a ball bearing screwed to the bottom of the bit and rides along an edge as the router progresses.

Routers are divided into two categories based on how the adjustment of the bit relative to the base plate is made.

On *fixed-base routers*, the motor is twisted in the base to raise and lower the bit. A thumbscrew tightens and locks it into position before use.

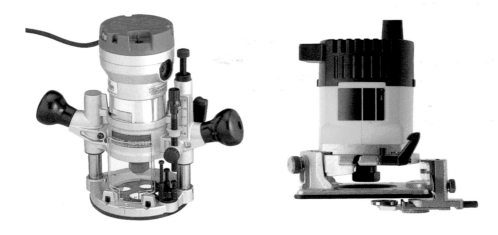

Plunge routers have a base that allows the motor and bit to be moved up and down during a cut. An adjustable stop limits how far down the bit can be pushed to establish the maximum depth of the cut. A lever locks the spring-loaded base in place and releases it to allow the bit to be retracted up and out of the wood. The fact that a cut can be started or stopped in the middle of a board makes the plunge router the more versatile of the two.

Other variations between the two types of routers include the presence of a pair of knob handles on the base, with an on/off switch on top of the motor. More advanced models have a trigger grips or D-shaped handles with built-in switches. Horsepower (hp) ratings range from small, ½ hp laminate trimmers, up to 3 hp monsters used for serious production work. A 1½ hp motor is sufficient for most home-based woodwork jobs.

Combination kits include one motor and both types of base. The kits are notably pricier than buying a router with a single base, but then cheaper than buying two separate routers.

A router is used just as if drawing with a pen. An average job can be achieved by working freehand, but more precise results may call for a straightedge or other guides. For this purpose, accessories to the router include *edge guides,* which help produce a parallel cut to an edge. *Guide bushings* are for tracing templates. Homemade and store-bought fences can also help you to rout in straight lines.

A *router table* will hold the router on a rigid stand, allowing small or complex pieces to be pushed against the bit rather than maneuvering the tool around them. This makes the process safer and provides more control with the cut.

Hand plane

Materials: **Wood**
Price: **$–$$**
Necessity: **OOO**
Skill level: **OOO**

Traditionally, if you wanted to shape, finish, or size a piece of wood beyond what could be achieved with a saw, or a drawknife, a variety of *hand plane* would be used. Today, most shaping and finishing tasks that were once accomplished with a type of plane can be done with much less time, effort and skill using commonly available machine tools.

Practice is necessary to become proficient at using planes, but in the hands of a skilled user, planes can deliver results equal to or superior to those achieved by more contemporary tools. In some cases, a hand plane is still the best tool for the job. How much planing work you choose to perform by hand is up to you, but it pays to have a feel for traditional tools because many modern tools are based on principles of their design and use.

The heart of a hand plane is its cutting edge. When all works well, the bottom of the plane (or sole) slides across the work piece, while the cutting edge protruding

from it shears off the tops of any high spots. The sliced-off material passes into the body of the plane through an opening in the sole called the throat. There it begins to curl and is ejected at the top of the plane. On wooden planes, the body is a block of wood with an angled pocket cut into the top. The iron rests against the back side of the pocket and is held tightly in place with a wooden wedge. To adjust the depth of the cut, the front (the toe) or rear (the heel) of the body is given a sharp tap. Not very scientific, but it does work. Japanese-style planes are also adjusted in this way.

The origins of the hand plane are fuzzy. By the time Pompeii was buried in 79 CE, the Romans had developed the tool and it is known that they used planes made of wood and metal because these have been excavated from the ruins of the city. By the Middle Ages, planes were made entirely from wood, except for the cutting iron, and they remained this way right up until

domestic plane production began in America in the early 1800s.

In 1870, the Stanley tool company began marketing an easily adjusted, all-metal plane invented by Leonard Bailey. The design, with its revolutionary blade, its adjustment system, and iron sole, was the pre-cursor to the modern Bailey-style planes produced today. The depth could be adjusted by simply turning a knurled knob. Pushing a lever adjusted the blade laterally and a cover piece with a simple cam lock held everything in place. At first they were expensive compared to wooden planes, but as mass production became more efficient, the wooden plane makers were priced out of business.

The *transitional plane* also appeared about this same period. It was a hybrid of the wooden and iron plane, used the Bailey adjustment mechanism but had a wooden sole. It offered the earlier Bailey adjustability while still affording the smooth wood-on-wood feel only a wooden sole can offer. Their moderate pricing when compared to the all-metal planes did not hinder their success either. Today it is possible to find transitional planes at flea markets and antique dealers.

Only a few types of metal hand planes are widely available new. Specialty woodworking tool manufacturers offer specialized planes, but otherwise finding used or antique planes is the best option for acquiring hand planes.

Block plane

Materials: **Wood**
Price: **$**
Necessity: **OOOO**
Skill level: **OO**

A *block plane* is a small hand plane used primarily for planing end-grain work, but it also performs well on other small-scale shaping and fitting jobs. Its compact size fits comfortably into the palm of the hand and is therefore also convenient to carry and store in a toolbox.

There are few differences between the block plane and other Bailey-style planes (see page 135) other than size. Most planes have irons held in place at an angle of 45° to the sole, with the bevel of the cutting edge facing downward. They also have an additional curved piece screwed to the top of the cutting iron known as a cap iron. It breaks the wood shavings as they enter the plane's throat and helps it run smoothly.

A standard block plane has its cutting iron positioned at around 21°. *Low-angle block planes* have irons set at around 13°. On both types the bevel on the cutting iron faces up—neither has a cap iron. Moving the bevel up allows the iron to sit at a shallower angle so that the cutting edge acts more like a knife blade, shearing across the grain. Since the severed end-grain is very weak, no cap iron is needed to break up the shavings. Eliminating the cap iron makes for an easier-to-use tool.

Like other Bailey planes, block planes use a knob to adjust the cutting depth and a lever to adjust the iron laterally. High-quality block planes feature an adjustable sole to vary the width of the throat and thereby fine-tune the amount of wood removed.

SAFETY FIRST
When storing a block plane, just be sure that other tools in the box don't shift around and nick the blade. Store the plane in an old, thick sock when it's not in use to ensure the blade is protected

Surfacing plane

Materials: **Wood**
Price: **$$**
Necessity: **OOO**
Skill level: **OOO**

The *jointer, jack* and *smoothing planes* are Bailey-style planes (see page 135) and are identical to each other except for their length and width—the key to their function.

The jointer plane is used to make an edge of a board straight and smooth. It is the longest hand plane (22 to 24 inches) you can buy. Its long sole rides over imperfections, bridging them, and trimming down any high spots until the surface is smooth. A shorter plane will not make the bridge over such surface imperfections and the result would be a smooth but distorted edge. Most edge preparation is now performed on a powered jointer (see page 140), but the hand plane can sometimes be the best option for pieces that are too long or awkward to maneuver onto the machine.

A jack plane is 14 or 15 inches long and is suited for preparing the face of a board if it is twisted or cupped, and needs flattening to be usable. It involves planing off the high spots and trimming down to a consistent thickness. For this task, it is beneficial to have a plane that is able to closely follow the contours of the board, which the shorter, narrower sole of the jack plane allows. Today, lumber is usually purchased already surfaced, but materials bought rough sawn or that may be deformed after surfacing, do still need some preparation.

A *powered thickness planer* is a contemporary alternative tool for this task, but initial work with a jack plane is often required to make the stock flat enough to run through the powered planer.

Smoothing planes are shorter still at 9 to 14 inches, and are generally the choice of tool for the final finishing of an already flat board. A practiced hand can work to make the surface of the wood as smooth as glass.

Spokeshave

Materials: **Wood**
Price: **$$**
Necessity: **OOO**
Skill level: **OO**

A *spokeshave* is used to shape curves and contours around the edge of a piece of wood. It does this by slicing away shavings, similar to the process of a plane. But where a plane has a long sole that wants to travel in a straight line, the very short sole of a spokeshave allows it to follow through and smooth out both tight and shallow curves. The handles on either side allow the user to maintain an even pressure on the sole and on the cutting edge as the cut progresses.

The spokeshave's cutting iron works just like a small plane iron. A cap iron for chip-breaking is screwed on top and the cutting edge protrudes through a throat in the narrow sole. High-quality spokeshaves feature a screw-type blade adjustment. A pair of screws with knurled heads hook into the blade and threading them in or out sets the depth of the cut.

The spokeshave can be handled by pulling or pushing, whichever gives the user the best control over the tool.

Most spokeshaves have flat soles with straight cutting edges. But curved soles are also available for better performance on concave surfaces.

Rasp plane

Materials: **Wood**
Plastic
Plaster
Drywall
Fiberglass
Price: **$**
Necessity: ⬡⬡⬡⬡
Skill level: ⬡

The *rasp plane* is commonly known as a Surform™, taken from the trademark of the Stanley tool company which developed the instrument in the 1950s. Its cutting action combines the qualities of a rasp (see page 131) and a plane (see page 134) to work like a heavy-duty cheese grater for roughly shaping a variety of materials.

The tool consists of a metal screen that is perforated with hundreds of holes arranged like the teeth of a rasp. At the edge of each hole is a sharp cutting edge. The screen is clipped to a hollow steel frame. Different size screens and frames are available. The screen's tiny cutting edges act as hundreds of small planes and slice off curls of material. This waste, called "swarf," passes through the holes and collects in the frame.

Because a rasp plane, or Surform™, is sharper than a rasp and less likely to clog, it works faster and it can be used on materials that would be dulled or damaged by a hand plane. However, its aggressive cut requires further finishing with files or sandpaper, once the basic form is achieved. When shaping wood, a sharp hand plane, chisel or spokeshave is often a faster, cleaner option.

TOP TOOL TIP
When the screen becomes dull or damaged, discard and replace it.

Jointer

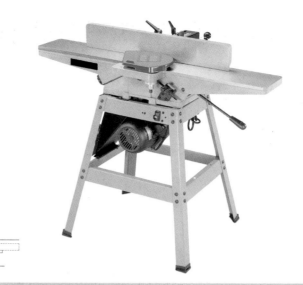

Materials: **Wood**
Price: **$$$$**
Necessity: **OO**
Skill level: **OOO**

1

The *jointer* is a large, motorized tool to make an edge or face of a board straight and flat. It performs the same function as the jack and jointer planes (see page 137).

As you look at the jointer, imagine it is a huge hand plane turned upside down. It has a long bed with a cutter in the middle, but there the similarities end. It has three blades, called knives, screwed into slots in the motorized, cylindrical, cutter head.

The bed is divided into two; the outfeed table and infeed table. The outfeed table is set level with the edge of the knives. The infeed table is adjustable in height and set slightly lower than the outfeed table. The difference in height between the two determines how much wood is removed from the board (*see figure 1*). The board slides along the infeed table until it hits the cutter head, which takes off material. The slightly narrower board slides onto the outfeed table. An adjustable guide "fence" keeps the board straight and square to the table edge throughout the cut.

Multiple passes may be necessary to obtain a perfect edge. Afterward, the board can be run through a bandsaw to trim the parallel opposite edge.

The jointer also dresses the faces of a board if board is cupped or twisted or the surface is marred. However, the width of the board is limited by the width of the jointer. While the jointer will smooth both faces of the board, it won't necessarily make them parallel to each other. For this you need to use a thickness planer (see page 137) or do it the old-fashioned way with a hand plane.

Jointers are sized by the widths of the cutting knives, and are available in 4-, 6-, and 8-inch widths. Six-inch models are most common; 4-inch jointers are useful for small pieces, but too small for furniture projects; 8-inch models are used in professional shops. Other than size and build quality, the differences are the manner the adjustments are made.to the cutter head, guide fence and infeed table.

Thickness planer

Materials: **Wood**
Price: **$$$$**
Necessity: **OO**
Skill level: **OOO**

A *thickness planer* is a motorized tool used to plane wood to a consistent thickness, and ensure both faces of the board are precisely parallel. Prior to the bench-top-sized versions, planers were large, bulky machines out of the price range of most hobbyist woodworkers. Stock had to be bought ready planed to standard thickness, or the alternative was to laboriously work rough stock by hand using a hand plane (see page 134).

The introduction of small, relatively portable planers enabled woodworkers to buy less expensive rough sawn lumber up to sizes of 12 inches wide and 6 inches deep, and plane the stock to a custom thickness, rather than relying on the standard sizes of presurfaced lumber.

The planer consists of a carriage assembly, which raises and lowers over a flat bed. Adjacent to the bed are flush-mounted infeed and outfeed tables that provide a surface for board to rest on. The carriage above the bed holds the motor, a cutter head with a pair of long, sharp cutting knives, and a pair of feed rollers to pull the board through the machine. The board slides across the infeed table and bed, beneath the cutter, and out the other side. The height of the carriage can be adjusted so the spinning cutters can slice off a very thin amount from the surface of a board. After each pass, the carriage is dropped a little lower until the desired thickness is achieved. A gauge on the side of the planer indicates how high the carriage is set.

The benchtop planer will not correct bowed or twisted pieces of wood; one side must first be flattened, using a jointer or bench plane. Then the flat side slides along the bed and the benchtop planer mills the opposite side to match.

Wood lathe and turning tools

Materials: **Wood**
Price: **$$–$$$$**
Necessity: ⬡⬡⬡
Skill level: ⬡⬡⬡

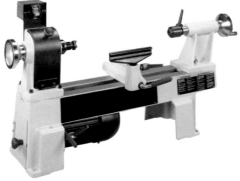

A *lathe* works in a similar way to a potter's wheel. A spinning base holds a piece of material that is shaped into a round form as pressure, and shaping tools are applied to it. Lathes are used to shape metal in machine shops and will mill pieces to a high degree of accuracy. Wood lathes are simpler; the material is easier to work and less precision is required than for machine parts.

Pretty much anything that is round and made of wood, from a baseball bat to a salad bowl, will have been shaped (or turned) on a lathe. There are two ways to use a lathe dependent on how the work piece is held by the machine.

The foundation of a lathe is a long, heavy casting called the bed, to which all the other components are attached. At either end of the bed is the headstock and the tailstock. The headstock is fixed in position on the user's left and contains the motor and a tapered chuck. The tailstock, on the user's right, holds a second chuck

and can be moved along the bed to accommodate different size work. Each chuck holds a pointed device called a center. Clamped to the bed between the two stocks is a T-shaped tool rest that comes with the lathe.

The method by which a baseball bat is turned is known as spindle turning, where the wood is held parallel to the bed by two centers. Various cutting tools can then be used to cut a profile along it as it spins. The length of the lathe's bed determines the maximum distance between the centers, and thereby the maximum length of the wood that can be turned.

A salad bowl or other vessels are examples of face turning, in which only one side of the object is held by the lathe. The tailstock is moved out of the way and the center is removed from the headstock. The bottom of the work piece is attached to a thick, round, steel plate with screws or special high-strength tape. On the bottom of the plate is a threaded ring that can be

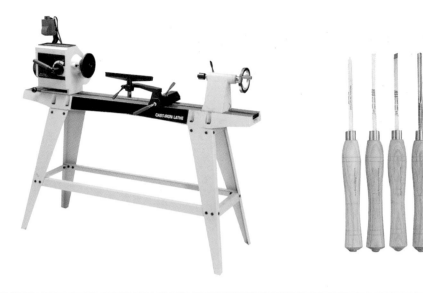

screwed onto the headstock's chuck. Holding the work this way allows the tool to be used on all sides of the work piece, not just the edge.

How large a bowl can be produced depends on how much space there is between the center of the chuck and the bed. On a wood lathe where this measures 6 inches, the salad bowl would be turned to a little shy of 12 inches diameter. The maximum diameter that can be turned over the bed is called the swing. For larger pieces, some lathes have an additional chuck on the other side of the motor to turn outboard, beyond the bed. A reasonably hefty machine with an additional tool rest are necessary to do so.

Lathes fall into three size categories and each size suits a different scale of work. *Mini* lathes are small enough to be portable. They work well for tiny projects such as pens, tops or parts for models or miniatures. Full-size lathes can handle material up to about 40 inches long and have a swing of 12 to 16 inches. In between the two are *midi* lathes. These typically have about 10 inches of swing and have 14 to 15 inches available between centers. They are small enough to be mounted to a bench top, but they weigh in at around 85 pounds apiece.

The wood lathe is just part of the equation. Its task is to hold and spin the stock. A set of turning tools is required to actually shape the material. There are four types: gouges, scrapers, skew chisels, and parting tools. While they share the same names as other woodworking tools, lathe tools are specialized and suitable only for turning work. Similarly, scrapers, chisels and gouges discussed elsewhere cannot be used on a lathe. Each turning tool has a long blade and handle, but the profile of the blade and the shapes of the tips differ. With each, the handle is held close to the body by the dominant hand while the other hand guides the tip of the tool along the tool rest.

Benchtop sander

Materials: **Wood**
Metal
Plastic
Price: **$$$**
Necessity: **○○○**
Skill level: **○**

Benchtop sanders are powered, stationary, sanding tools. Handheld sanders are used for finishing work, and while benchtop sanders leave a reasonably smooth edge, they are most often used for shaping. A fairly course abrasive quickly removes material from wood, metal, and plastic.

Belt sanders, like their portable cousins, use a wide loop of sandpaper that runs continuously around a set of parallel drums. Some models orientate the belt vertically, with an exposed portion running down past the edge of a small table, on which to hold a work piece. This makes it easy to shape small parts and to hold them at a precise angle to the belt. Alternatively, in other models, the belt runs horizontally and has a fence on one end to hold the work in place, and this position is better suited to large pieces. Further, some models are adjustable and the belt can be pivoted and locked in either position.

Disc sanders use a round adhesive sanding disc adhered to a stiff, motorized backup plate, which is mounted perpendicularly to the floor. Beside it is a work support table similar to the vertical belt sander. A good choice for home shops is a combination machine, which has both a 6-inch wide belt and a 9-inch diameter disc powered by a single motor.

Oscillating spindle sanders are a third group of benchtop sanders used for sanding and shaping pieces with tight inside and outside curves. They consist of an enclosed housing with a flat table on top. A cylindrical sanding drum spins and oscillates up and down through the center of the table. The vertical movement of the drum extends the life of the abrasive sleeve by using its full height.

An accessory drum sander for a drill press is an inexpensive alternative to a spindle sander which may be used only occasionally. It does not have the same oscillating motion, but it can reach parts of the work piece that a disc or belt sander cannot.

Bench grinder

Materials: **Metal**
Kits: **Machine and metal work**
Price: **$$**
Necessity: **OOO**
Skill level: **OO**

The *bench grinder* is designed to be mounted securely to a workbench or a dedicated tool stand. It consists of an electric motor with a round grindstone, wire brush, or buffing wheel attached to each end of a central shaft. Each wheel has a protective guard with an opening, leaving about one-third of the wheel exposed. At the bottom of this opening is a tool rest to support the work piece, and above it is a clear polycarbonate eye shield to protect the user from sparks and debris.

The grindstone is a hard disc of man-made abrasive used to shape metal, to reshape bevels on chisels and lathe tools, and to sharpen awls, drill bits, and garden tools. Grindstones of different degrees of coarseness are available.

When a grindstone becomes grooved or clogged, an accessory *wheel dresser* is used to scour the surface of the wheel to restore its abrasion capability.

Wire brush wheels are available in different grades of coarseness. They remove rust, scale, or corrosion from the surface of metal. The wire wheel will restore the surface of all but the most pitted metals, but beware—some of the coarser versions can scour away the metal itself. If you have antique tools or any collectors' items to restore, think twice before cleaning them with a wire wheel. A freshly brushed surface can seriously diminish their desirability.

Buffing wheels will restore the polished finish on solid and plated metal. Buffs are composed of several layers of cloth stacked up and sewn together to make a soft wheel. A rigid arbor in the center of the stack provides a way to mount the wheel on the grinder. Rubbing compound is applied to the buff and the work piece is held against it as it spins. There are several different combinations of buffs and compounds for polishing, so it is important to be certain of what treatment the item you are polishing requires in order to avoid damaging it.

145

Rotary tool

Materials: **Wood**
Plastic
Metal
Glass
Tile
Price: **$$**
Necessity: **ooo**
Skill level: **oo**

A *rotary tool* is a small, handheld, motorized device used for detailed grinding and shaping work on a variety of materials. Like a router (see page 132), it is little more than a motor with a collet to hold bits. It is very similar to a high-speed dental drill in that a single power unit is used to drill, grind, shape, and polish, depending on which bit is used. Also like the dental drill, the rotary's high speeds (up to 35,000 rpm) allow it to cut effectively with the slightest pressure applied.

A dizzying array of bits is available to tackle a variety of jobs—from manicures to sharpening a lawn-mower blade. Among these are are little wire brushes and cut-off wheels, discs, and drums for sanding and polishing, rasp-toothed and abrasive grinding tips, tools for carving wood, and cutting and engraving glass and tile.

A basic rotary tool will operate at one or two different motor speeds. Bits perform better at different speeds, so advanced models have speed adjustments.

The rotary tool is simple to use, but practice and dexterity in selecting the best bit and motor speed, and getting a feel for the right pressure and feed rate for a particular job go far toward achieving the best results.

Corded and rechargeable models are available. Most are sold in kits that include the rotary tool, a range of basic bits, a collet wrench, a storage case, and user's instructions, and additional bits can be purchased separately. A wide range of accessories allows you to use the rotary tool as a tiny router or drill press or will tailor the tool for most any specific task.

Taps and dies

Materials: **Metal**
Plastic
Wood
Kits **Machine and metal work**
Price: **$–$$**
Necessity: **OOO**
Skill level: **OO**

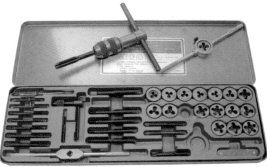

Taps and *dies* are used to cut threads into pieces of metal, plastic, or dense wood so that a nut or bolt with machine threads can be screwed into or onto them. They can also restore damaged threads of a screw, nut, bolt, or machine part that is stripped or mashed in the middle of a repair job. Taps and dies are bought in sets that include a range of sizes of each and a pair of handles. Pieces can also be bought individually.

Taps cut the threads on the *inside* of a predrilled hole. There are many different sizes of threads, and many different sizes of holes. However, each individual tap will cut threads of one size in holes of one particular diameter. This is why it makes sense to buy them in a set, to be prepared for whatever combinations arise.

A tap is made from a hard, high-speed steel shank. One end is ground to a square shape and clamped into a special handle used to turn the tap. The other end is cross-shaped and threaded. Shavings

accumulate in the voids between the arms of the cross as the tap is twisted into the hole and waste material is cut away.

When repairing a thread, the tap is carefully screwed into the existing threads to clear and straighten the damage.

Dies cut threads on the *outside* of a bolt or rod. A die is a thick, round disc with a threaded hole in the center. Three or four holes around it provide a space for shavings to gather. The die is placed in its own special handle and is held in place with set screws. Like taps, each die will only cut one thread size on material of one particular diameter.

When using a tap or die, be sure to select the correct size to match the hole or rod you are cutting. It's important not to cut too much at once, and typically, it is best to make one half-turn with the tool at a time, and then back it off a quarter-turn to break the shavings. It is also essential to keep the tool well lubricated with oil throughout the thread-cutting process.

Driving and prying

Animals, especially humans, have been hammering on things throughout their evolution. Even otters use rocks as hammers to break open shells! Driving and prying is a basic and uncomplicated instinct, but there is a knack or technique to it, and using the right tools, and taking good care of them, are both important parts of achieving safe and satisfactory results.

General rules
- Never bang two striking tools together, as you can chip or crack one or both.

- Check a tool over before use. If its handle is loose, it should be repaired to make safe, or maybe replaced, otherwise the head may fly off during use. Also, if any part of a hammer appears cracked, it is unsafe and should be discarded.

- If the face of a hammer or end of a chisel is mushroomed over from repeated blows, the burred edges should be filed back to solid material. These loose bits of steel at the edge of the tool can shoot off when struck, creating dangerous shrapnel.

- Wear eye protection to guard against chipped tools and any flying debris.

Beginner's class

Using a hammer sounds pretty simple in theory, but then again, so does tennis and golf. In each case, there are certain grips and swings that deliver optimum results.

1 Hold the hammer an inch or two from the end of the handle and grasp it as though you are 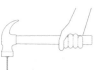 shaking hands with it. Hold the handle firmly, but not too tight; a death-grip on the hammer will only make your hand tired. The swing should be a continuous fluid motion and your arm should bend at the elbow, not at the wrist. Be confident and allow the full weight of the hammer's head come down on the nail. Don't try to pull back or stop it at the last second—the nail will take care of that. It's the momentum of the head that drives the nail deeper into the wood. Pulling back or holding the handle close to the head will rob the hammer of this momentum, requiring more swings to do the job.

2 Before you start pounding away, it's helpful to use a couple of lighter blows to get the nail started straight and able to

- Hold a hammer near the end of the handle and grasp as though you are shaking hands with it, but do not hold the handle too tight. The swing should be a continuous fluid motion. Strike items squarely. Avoid glancing blows, which can damage the tool and the item being driven.

- Make sure the work is firmly supported and is not flexing or deforming when a blow is applied.

- To avoid marring the surface of an exposed trim piece, stop short of sinking a nail all the way with a hammer. Use a nail set to drive it flush with the surface or to sink it below so that it can be filled.

- If you bend a nail when driving it in, pull it out and start again with a fresh one.

Once a nail is bent, any following blows from a hammer will bend it right over.

- When prying or pulling nails, place a scrap block of wood under the tool to avoid damaging the material beneath it. This will also give the leverage needed to pull long nails.

- When removing nails from trim to be reused, use a pair of tongue-and-groove pliers or end-cutting pliers (see pages 176 and 70) to pull out through the back side of the material, to avoid splitting the exposed face.

stand on its own. While doing this, it is necessary to hold the nail with your free hand. When starting out, you may want to hold it as shown, rather than pinching the nail between your fingertips. If you do happen to miss the nail and hit your fingers, it hurts a little less this way.

3 When you use a curved claw hammer to pull nails, place a thin scrap of wood beneath the hammer to avoid

denting or marring the surface of the work piece. This works well if the nail's head is down close to the surface of the work piece, but if the nail has already been pulled out most of the way, it can be tricky to get enough leverage to pull out the last portion. In this case, use a thicker block of wood under the hammer. This will raise the hammer of the surface of the work piece and give you the added leverage needed to remove the nail.

Mallet

Materials: **Wood**
Metal
Plastic
Price: **$**
Necessity: ⬡⬡⬡⬡
Skill level: ⬡

When assembling a project, and the parts need to be "persuaded" into place, there are two options: you can either hit it with a metal hammer, which may dent or damage it, or you can use a *mallet*.

Mallets, unlike hammers, have a head and a handle made of a resilient material that is less likely to mar the surface of a work piece. The simplest mallets have heads made from a coil of raw hide or a block of soft rubber. More advanced types, with replaceable rubber and plastic faces, use a steel head to provide additional mass in a compact form.

One of the most useful is the *dead blow mallet*, with its head and handle molded from a single piece of soft, reinforced plastic. The head is hollow and filled with oil and lead shot. When other soft-face mallets hit a surface, they have a tendency to rebound. Not so with the dead blow mallet. The oil and shot inside the head dampen the impact and thereby minimize any bounce.

A mallet can be used to shape sheet metal over a rigid wood or metal form, but it should only be used to strike broad surfaces, as impact on a small point can cause material to punch into the surface of the head and damage it.

Mallets for chisels

Materials: **Wood**
Plastic
Price: **$**
Necessity: **OOO**
Skill level: **OO**

Wooden-headed mallets are used to strike wood chisels and gouges.

There are two types of mallets commonly used with chisels. A *joiner's mallet* has a large rectangular head with a broad striking face made from a block of solid or laminated hardwood. The wooden head is attached to a separate handle, like a hammer, but it provides a much more forgiving blow than a hammer's metal head. Its large striking area makes it easier to hit the chisel.

A *carver's mallet* has a round handle and head created from one single piece of wood that is usually turned from very dense hardwood such as cocobolo or lignum vitae (the only wood that sinks), for heft and durability. Its compact size makes it easy to work with a chisel in an odd position, which occurs when carving. It is held by the handle for heavy blows and grasped by the head for light ones.

As a general rule, the handles of chisels, gouges, and other carving tools should not be struck with a metal hammer, as the hammer's hard face will mushroom the end of a wooden handle and eventually cause it to split. Some plastic-handled chisels have protective caps to withstand a hammer blow, but a mallet is the preferable tool to use.

The names of the different mallets are not specific to the task involved, and you should feel free to use whichever type feels more comfortable. Avoid using a chisel mallet to drive nails or to strike metal items, and it will last a lifetime.

Tack hammer

Materials:	**Wood**
	Metal
Kits:	**Apartment**
	Home
	Craft
Price:	**$**
Necessity:	**OOO**
Skill level:	**O**

The *tack hammer* is the tool to use to drive tacks or small nails. To drive in a small nail, the nail is best held pinched between the thumb and forefinger. The hammer taps it in far enough for it to stand on its own, when fingers can be moved safely out of the way, and the nail is ready to be driven fully into position. The difficulty with small nails is that they are often smaller than fingertips so that a wide-faced hammer will likely strike your thumb instead of the nail, with pain and some cursing to follow. A tack hammer is slim enough to avoid these difficulties.

Tack hammers have a slim, wooden handle and a light, compact head with a squarish face. The side of the head opposite the face tapers to a wedge or to an even smaller face, depending on the style of hammer. The small end is used to start the nail because it is small enough to slip between the fingertips as it comes down on the nail head. After a few taps, the nail can be released from the fingers,

the hammer is flipped around and the larger face is used to drive home the nail. Some tack hammers have a magnetic face that will hold the head of a nail in place, taking fingers right out of the equation.

TOP TOOL TIP
If you're without a tack hammer, poke a nail or tack through the corner of a scrap piece of cardboard and hold the cardboard instead. Hammer the tack in part way, tear off the card, then finish.

Claw hammer

Materials: **Wood**
Metal
Kits: **Apartment**
Home
Price: **$**
Necessity: **⬡⬡⬡⬡⬡**
Skill level: **⬡**

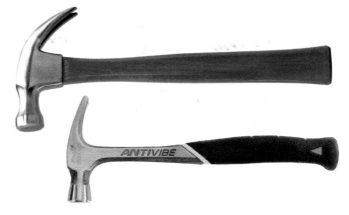

There are two types of *claw hammer:* the *curved claw*, and the *straight*, or *ripping, claw*. The curved claw is the more common and is the choice for general use as it is the more adept at pulling out nails. The straight claw hammer, or *framing hammer*, is used for rough carpentry, on walls and roofs, and works better for prying and ripping involved in rough framing or demolition.

There are two styles of hammer face, smooth and checkered. Both faces have a slight crown and beveled edge, but while the smooth face is, well, smooth, the checkered face has a waffle pattern forged into it to give some traction that helps prevent glancing blows. The downside is that when the nail is fully sunk, a waffle-shaped pattern can be left in the work surface, which is not too much of a problem in concrete formwork, but not ideal in finished millwork.

For as many sizes of nails, there are almost as many sizes of hammer. They are measured by and differ in the weight of their heads, which ranges from 7 to 32 ounces. A 16-ounce hammer is ideal for most uses. There are also a number of handle styles to choose from. The traditional handle is made from hickory, a strong, resilient, straight-grained wood. The end of the handle passes through a hole in the head called the "eye" and has wedges driven into it to hold the head in place. A modern method is to epoxy the wood handle in place, making it less likely to loosen over time. Handles are most commonly made from fiberglass and other composites which are strong, rot-resistant, and lighter than wood. Some have shock-dampening qualities, which can be an important consideration if the tool is for repetitive occupational use. A third style is the steel handle, forged as a single piece along with the head. A grip made from rubber or stacked leather washers encases the handle. Steel hammers are very well balanced and extremely durable.

Nail set

Materials: **Wood**
Metal
Price: **$**
Necessity: ⬡⬡⬡⬡
Skill level: ⬡

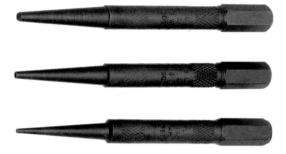

Most interior millwork, such as baseboards and door and window casings, are nailed into place using finish nails, which have very small heads. A *nail set* can be used to sink (or set) such heads about $\frac{1}{16}$ inch below the surface of the surrounding wood. The resultant small indentation is then filled with wood putty and can be painted over to completely conceal the nail. It is invaluable for driving nails into awkward or hard-to-reach positions. The nail set can provide just enough extra length to finish driving the nail.

A nail set is a single piece of steel about 4 inches long with a square head, a knurled midsection and a base tapering to a round tip. The diameter of the tip varies from $\frac{1}{32}$ to $\frac{3}{16}$ inch and it may be flat, pointed, or cupped. Nail sets are sold individually and in sets of three.

To sink a nail, first select a set with a tip equal to or smaller than the width of the nail head. (A larger set would make an unnecessarily large hole.) Hold the set between thumb and three fingers and place the tip on the head of the nail. Keep the set in line with the nail and drive it in with a few taps. Avoid tipping the set or it may slip off the nail and damage the adjacent wood.

Ball peen hammer

Materials: **Metal**
Kits: **Machine and metal work**
Price: **$**
Necessity: **OOOO**
Skill level: **O**

Just as a claw hammer is *the* hammer for those who work with wood, the *ball peen hammer* is *the* hammer for metal workers. Its rounded face is used to shape metal, while its flat face is used to drive punches and dies or to tap parts into place. It is also designed to strike cold chisels, which are short, hexagonal steel bars with a beveled tip used to split or shear metal.

The rounded face of the hammer, opposite the flat face, is the ball peen. It can be used in the initial stages of shaping a concave surface and to apply a "hammered," or evenly dimpled, finish across the surface of a work piece. It is also used to install small rivets to fasten metal parts together without the use of welds, screws, or bolts. A rivet has a round metal shank and a preformed head on one end. The shank is passed through holes in the pieces to be joined so that the head rests on one side of the assembly. The hammer is then used to "peen over" the free end of the rivet, mushrooming it so

that the parts are squeezed tightly together and the rivet cannot be pulled back through the hole. The end of the rivet is first flattened with the face, then the edges are hammered over with the peen.

Ball peen hammers are available with heads ranging from 4 to 48 ounces, sized for different scales of work.

Sledge hammer

Materials: **Stone**
Concrete
Masonry
Price: **$**
Necessity: **OOO**
Skill level: **OO**

Sledge hammers deliver heavy blows that are required when working with cold chisels to cut stone, masonry, and concrete, or to drive spikes and stakes, or to knock pieces apart during major demolition work.

The heads of sledge hammers can range in size from 6 to 16 pounds. For durability, they are forged from hardened and tempered steel and have slightly crowned faces milled onto them. Handles around 3 feet long allow the hammer to be swung like an axe to deliver maximum power. Some handles have an additional protective sleeve just below the head to help prevent damage should the head accidentally miss the target and the handle slams into it instead.

Between the largest sledge hammers are the hand drilling and engineer's hammers. These have heads similar to the sledge but on a smaller scale, 2 to 4 pounds typically. Hand-drilling hammers, also called stone cutter's hammers, are around 11 inches long and more the size of claw hammers. They are used to strike cold chisels and star drills to manually cut and drill stone and masonry. Engineer's hammers are longer, at 14 to 16 inches, and offer more power than the drilling hammer and more control than the sledge.

Prybar

Materials: **Wood**
Price: **$**
Necessity: **OOO**
Skill level: **OO**

When doing renovation work, selective demolition is usually part of the early stages of the project. This involves carefully removing pieces or components in such a way they can be reused, or in such a way to limit the damage to areas surrounding them. *Prybars* are the best tools for "surgically" removing millwork, framing and flooring, piece by piece.

A *cat's paw prybar* will extract deeply embedded nails. On one end is a sharp, curved "paw" with a notch cut in the tip. A claw hammer is used to drive the tip down into the wood beside the nail so that the notch hooks in beneath the nail head. The prybar is then levered to pull the nail out far enough to fit a larger tool on it and pull it the rest of the way.

A *flat bar prybar* removes moldings and trim, such as door casings. The thin flat tips can be tapped into a joint to open it up, and then the bar is pulled to the side to lever the pieces apart. The straight end of the bar prys the pieces free.

Sometimes less collateral damage is done if a board is split into pieces for removal, rather than taking it all out in one shot. The *ripping chisel* is a heavy-duty version of the flat bar, suitable for prying large objects, as well as splitting wood along the grain. Driving the chisel's sharp tips into the wood and twisting it usually causes board to split.

TOP TOOL TIP

Try to position a split so that it occurs at a fastener, to free the pieces on either side.

When pulling things apart, it helps to have an idea of how it was assembled in the first place. That way, you'll know where to look for fasteners and joints, the strong and weak points, and be better able to plan your approach.

Fastening

Assembly and disassembly of connections is a frequent task in most construction and maintenance jobs. In the past, tools for fastening items were the tools of the joiner, carpenter, and blacksmith. When mass-produced fasteners became widely available in the form of nails, screws, adhesives, etc., a range of new tools was spawned with which to utilize them, and the way everyday things were built was revolutionized for everyone. For both basic DIY work and for more ambitious projects, the type of fastener used to make a connection will dictate what tools are called for.

General rules
- To help prevent pull-out or malfunction of a fastener, use the correct type for the material. As a general rule, at least two-thirds of a fastener should engage the underlying material. Also, the more fasteners that are used, the less work each of them has to do.

Beginner's class

It's easy to figure out that you need a screwdriver to turn a screw and a wrench to turn a nut or bolt, but each tool comes in a variety of sizes. When instaling or removing a particular fastener it's important to use the size appropriate for the job. Otherwise, damage to the fastener or the tool is not only possible, but likely.

1 When selecting a screwdriver, choose one whose tip matches the size of the screw for which it will be used. It should fully engage the recess in the screw head and should not be too loose. If the tip is too small, it can twist or spin in the head,

Bad Good Bad

grinding off the edges of the recess. This makes it difficult for a screwdriver to grip the screw to turn it. Depending on the style of the screwdriver, an oversize slotted screwdriver may not grip properly, making it more likely to slip out, and the sides of the tip that hang out beyond the screw head will mar the work piece as the screw is drawn down snug. With an oversize Phillips™ bit, only the very tip will engage the recess. A hard screw will grind the tip right off a cheap screwdriver, or a strong screwdriver will ream out the top of the recess.

- Select a fastener large enough not to bend or break when in use.

- Make sure the fastener has enough bearing on the item being mounted to prevent it pulling through. Use a fastener with a wide head or add a washer if necessary.

- If you are making a structural connection, for example, attaching a deck to a house, all of these considerations are of vital importance. If you are unsure of whether a structural connection is adequate, consult an expert or a reference book.

- When hanging items on walls, especially heavy items, anchor directly to a wall stud when possible. See page 213 for electronic stud finders and other low-tech ways to locate studs.

- Pre-drill holes for screws, especially if they are to be located near the end of a piece of wood or in the end-grain. Holes should be large enough to remove excess material, but small enough to let the threads bite well.

- Where connections will be exposed to the elements, use corrosion-resistant fasteners or waterproof adhesives.

- Verify that adhesives are compatible with the materials being joined. Read the product labels and do a test on an inconspicuous area if you are unsure.

- Apply glue with a roller or a small brush and work evenly over a work piece to avoid weak spots in the finished joint. Wipe away any excess that oozes out of any of the joints, using a damp rag, before the glue dries. If glue is not cleaned up promptly, its residue can cause the part of the surface affected to finish entirely differently than its surrounding area.

---

2 With wrenches, it's difficult to use one too small, because it simply won't fit onto the fastener. The risk is in using one too large. Open-ended wrenches should slip securely over the flat faces of the nut or bolt head. Box-ended wrenches should neatly engage the corners of the fastener. A wrench too large means a loose fit, which makes it easier to round off the corners of the nut or bolt when force is applied to the wrench. A fastener damaged in this way is difficult to remove. It's a good idea to keep standard and metric wrenches separate, because it's easy to grab one that is a close fit, but not as good as it could be.

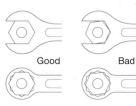

Good   Bad

3 When using a wrench with a movable jaw, such as a pipe wrench or an adjustable wrench, orient the wrench so that pressure is applied on the fixed, rigid jaw. Also, periodically check the wrench as you work to make sure the jaw hasn't loosened.

Nails

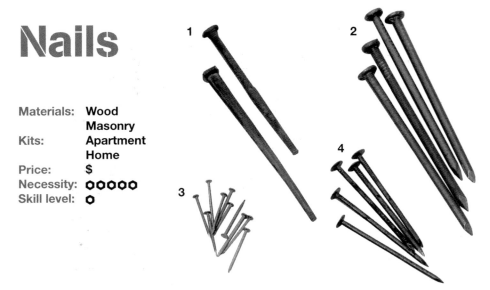

Materials: **Wood**
Masonry
Kits: **Apartment**
Home
Price: **$**
Necessity: ⬡⬡⬡⬡⬡
Skill level: ⬡

Metal nails have been made for thousands of years. Until the mid-eighteenth century, they were hand-forged, making them fairly expensive, while "tree nails," straight-grained wood pins, were used for more day-to-day applications. In the 1750s, a machine was developed which cut nails from metal plate. Their price reduced and they were more widely available. Improved mass-production further reduced their price in the 1800s, until, around the turn of the twentieth century when round nails made from wire were introduced, the price of nails dropped further.

The current designation of nail sizes stems from an old English system used when nails were hand-forged. A 3 inch-long nail is called a "10 penny" nail—historically, that was the price a blacksmith was paid to make one hundred 3-inch nails. Even more archaic, a 10 penny nail is noted in print as 10d, the "d" standing for *denarius*, a silver coin of ancient Rome, equal to ten asses! Nails between 1 and

6 inches long have a "penny" measure. Nails beyond this are described in inches. Nails longer than 6 inches are called *spikes* and can be as long as 12 inches for heavy-duty connections.

A nail stays in place due to friction between its shank and the surrounding wood fibers. The thicker the shank, the more area it has and the more friction is available to hold it. A thick nail with a sharp point will hold the best, but it may also split the wood. Tapping the tip of a nail to dull it will help to minimize splitting, as will using a slimmer nail.

Variations:
Nails differ in their materials and their coatings, aiding performance and corrosion resistance.
(1) *Cut nails.* The "closest living relative" to the nails produced in the 1800s. They are used to nail flooring in place. Special hardened versions are used for nailing into masonry. **(2)** *Common nails* have a flat

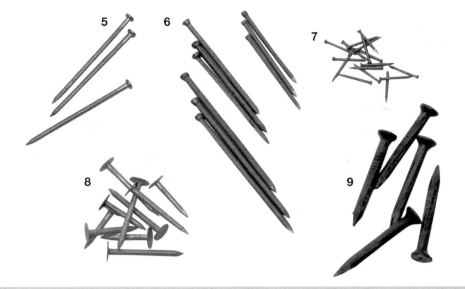

head and a round shank and are used for general construction. They are available in sizes from 2d to 60d (1 to 6 inches long). *Box nails* are slimmer versions of the common nail, which helps to minimize splitting. **(3)** *Wire nails* are the same shape as common nails, but shorter and finer. **(4)** *Sinker nails* are shaped like common nails and coated with a film of resin. Heat from friction generated when driving it melts the resin and helps to "glue" the nail in place. **(5)** *Ring shank*. Once a nail is sunk, rings cut up the shaft of the nail act as teeth. They dig into the surrounding wood. **(6)** *Finish nails* are used to nail exposed trim where little holding power is required. The small, cupped heads can be sunk below the surface of the wood using a nail set (see page 154). The resulting shallow indentation is filled, sanded and painted to conceal the nail. Finish nails are available from 2d to 20d (1 to 4 inches long), and shorter than 1 inch are called **(7)** *brads*. **(8)** *Galvanized roofing nails* are used to fasten asphalt shingle and roofing felt. The broad head makes the nail much less likely to pull through soft materials. *Duplex* or *scaffold nails*. These are very similar to common nails, except they have two heads. They are used for temporary construction such as formwork or shoring that has to be disassembled at a future point. The nail sinks up to its first head, leaving the second poking up where it can be grabbed by a prybar or claw hammer. *Escutcheon pins*. These short nails have a sharp tip and a polished oval head and are used when the nail is in an exposed location. An escutcheon is a trim ring, such as is found around a keyhole or around a radiator pipe there it comes up through the floor. **(9)** *Masonry nails* are used to nail into concrete, concrete block, and brick. They have a thick fluted shank and a sharp tip. A pilot hole must be drilled in the masonry beforehand.

Powered nailer

Materials: **Wood**
Price: **$**
Necessity: **OOO**
Skill level: **O**

Powered nailers are used to drive nails, brads, or staples with more speed and less effort than would be required to do the job by hand. Different sizes are used for each category of fastener. Large nailers are used for framing and roofing, and small ones will finish carpentry such as interior millwork and trim for baseboards or door casing, and craft work.

Most are pneumatically powered, which involves compressed air being supplied by a hose from a remote compressor to drive the nail. Other types of nailer operate on replaceable fuel cells as a power source, avoiding being tethered to a compressor while working. Small brad nailers and staplers are often electric-powered.

The nailer shoots fasteners from either a coiled or stick-shaped magazine. There are two parts to the firing system: a trigger on the handle and a spring-loaded foot on the nose. These work together in one of two ways. The *pull trigger* action will fire a nail every time the nose is pressed to the work piece. The *touch/pull* action requires the nose to touch the work piece *before* the trigger can be pulled to fire the nail. This is a safety feature as it reduces the risk of misfires and of driving two nails into one spot. Some nailers have a built-in micro-processor that disengages the firing mechanism if a nail is not driven within a certain period of time, making the tool safer still.

On many nailers, the magazine is mounted at an angle to the tip, to improve the tool's balance and make it easier to nail in tight corners. Nailers in general are capable of driving brads and nails ranging from ½ to 3½ inches in length. Each particular tool can usually handle a few sizes, with about a 1½ inch difference between the largest and smallest nails that will fit in the tool.

Flooring nailer

Materials: **Wood Flooring**
Price: **$$$$**
Necessity: O
Skill level: OO

A *flooring nailer* is specifically designed for nailing wood flooring into place over a plywood sub floor. Some models can be operated manually, while more advanced versions are pneumatically powered, by pressurized air supplied from a separate, remote compressor.

Wood strip flooring has a tongue milled into one edge and a matching groove milled into the other. As a strip is laid down, the groove of one strip fits over the tongue of the previous piece. It is then nailed in place before the next piece is installed. To conceal the nail from view, it is driven at a 45° angle through the tongue, where it is covered by the next strip of flooring.

Laying strip flooring requires two tools: a flooring nailer and a two-faced mallet. The firm mallet face is used to tap the strips into position. Once set, the nailer is hooked in place over the tongue of the flooring strip. A safety trigger on the handle is pulled and the other soft, rubber face of the mallet is then used to tap a pad on the nailer to activate it. Air pressure fires a barbed, L-shaped nail, called a cleat, through the tongue and into the sub floor. The process is repeated down the board to secure the strips.

The nailer can be adjusted to shoot the cleat at the correct angle and to just the right depth, making the process simple and quick. A built-in magazine holds a hundred or so nails which are glued together in a long strip. This arrangement simplifies reloading.

These are professional tools and expensive. Unless you intend to do a lot of flooring they may not be worth buying since they are widely available for rent.

Threaded fasteners

Materials: **Wood**
                   Metal
                   Plastic
Kits: **Apartment**
                   Home
Price: **$**
Necessity: **ooooo**
Skill level: **o**

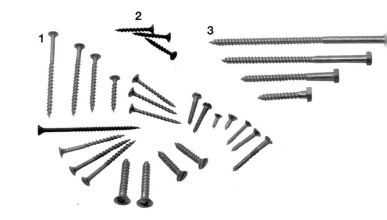

Threaded fasteners provide a more secure connection than nails because they have threads cut into their shanks. The thread cuts into the material to provide a mechanical grip, as opposed to nails, which rely on friction alone. When a material is too thin or difficult to thread into, threaded nuts are used to give the fastener something to engage instead. They are easily removed and replaced, unlike nails or adhesives. Endless sizes and varieties of fasteners are available, all with different combinations of heads, drive, and thread styles.

Steel is the most common material of manufacture, usually with a black or zinc finish to ward off corrosion. Chrome nickel and brass plating provide the attractive finishes. Fasteners made from brass and stainless-steel are best for exterior work.

The fastener's thread largely determines its use. Machine screws have fine, accurately cut thread and are designed to be used with nuts or in holes where matching thread has been cut (or tapped). Only hard and tough materials, such as metals and plastics, can support machine threads. Fine thread would tear out of soft materials, and for those, wood screws are used, which have a wide thread, providing a larger bite.

The size of a fastener cut with machine threads is measured by the diameter of its shank and how many threads it has per inch of length. The length is measured from the top of the head on flathead screws and from the underside of the head on other types.

Screw types:
(1) *Wood screws*. Used for wood-to-wood and metal-to-wood connections. Wood screws are described by their length and gauge, or thickness, number. Lengths vary from ¼ to 4 inches. Gauge varies from 0 to 20. **(2)** *Drywall screws* are wood screws especially designed for insertion with an electric drill or screw gun. The slim

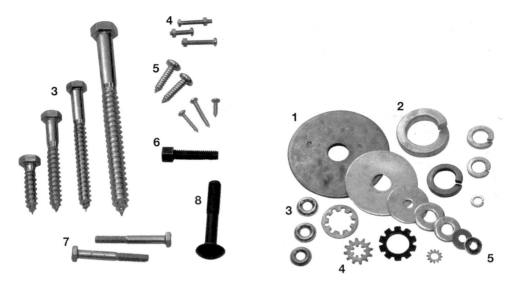

shank and sharp point allows them to grip into wood and sheet metal without pre-drilling. A black finish provides light corrosion resistance for interior work; galvanized finishes are available for exterior use. **(3)** *Lag screws* are like jumbo-size wood screws for mounting heavy fixtures. The shank and diameter are larger than regular wood screws and they have hex heads that can be turned with a wrench. **(4)** *Sheet metal screws*. A sharp point fastens sheet metal and wood without pre-drilling and coarse threads eliminate the need for a nut. Some points are specially designed to be self-drilling, aiding installation. **(5)** *Machine screws* have machine threads cut into them and are used for strong and precise connections in hard materials. Unless the screw is used in a threaded hole, a matching nut is required. **(6)** *Set screws* are machine screws with no head, but have a hexagonal recess in the end of the shank to takee an Allen wrench.

(7) *Cap screw/bolt*. Hex or socket heads allow cap screws to be held or tightened with a wrench, rather than a screwdriver. **(8)** *Carriage bolts* have a machine thread, and are used to connect a large wood component to a second wood or metal piece. They are used when an exposed fastener is necessary, but where a hex head would be unsuitable for aesthetic or security reasons. The head goes on the wood side, and the square neck is drawn down into the wood as the nut is tightened. The neck digs in, preventing the bolt from twisting, and leaves the smooth, round head exposed to view.

Washers

Washers are are disc-like pieces placed between the work piece and a nut or bolt head. They act as a distributor of the load that is applied by the fastener over a wider area and protect the surface of an item from being scratched or damaged as the nut is tightened.

Continued 165

Drive styles

- Slotted
- Phillips™
- Combination slotted/Phillips™
- Robertson, or Square Drive
- Torx™
- Clutch
- Allen
- Hex

Head styles

- Flat head
- Oval head
- Bugle head
- Round head
- Pan head
- Button head
- Socket head
- Hex head

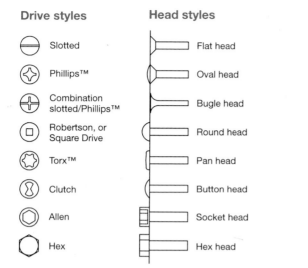

(1) *Fender washers* are broad with a disproportionately small center hole. They are used to distribute load over a wide area and provide a bearing point when a hole in a piece to be joined is too large. **(2)** *Spring lock washers* are split and slightly twisted to form a shallow spring that, when compressed during tightening, puts pressure on the nut to resist loosening. **(3)** *Countersunk/finish washers* are used under the head of flathead or oval-head screws, to provide an additional bearing area and a finished appearance while eliminating the need to countersink. **(4)** *Toothed lock washers* have teeth on the inside or outside that dig into the piece and the nut to hold it in place. **(5)** *Round washers* can be stacked to shim a part into position, locking the nut in place.

Nuts:

Nuts are cut with a machine thread and are used with matching bolts and screws. Using a nut means the screw's thread does not have to bite in either of the pieces being joined. The nut threads onto the end of the fastener, pinching the parts between itself and the fastener's head.
(1) *Square nuts.* The simplest of nuts has broad, flat faces that can be gripped by a wrench.
(2) *Hex nut* is the most commonly used and it has six sides instead of four. The extra facets allow a wrench to engage it at more positions than would a square nut, which is helpful when space is limited.
(3) *Lock nuts.* An integral ring of nylon at the end of the threads helps prevent the nut from loosening through vibration.
(4) *Acorn nuts.* A domed cover on the nut protects the ends of the threads and provides a finished appearance.
(5) *Wing nuts.* Two wings on either side of the nut allow it to be installed and removed by hand, without the use of a wrench.

Wall anchors

Materials: **Wood**
Masonry
Plastic
Kits: **Home**
Price: **$**
Necessity: **OOO**
Skill level: **O**

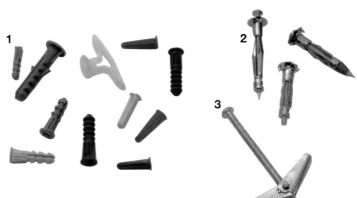

Sometimes a screw alone will not be sufficient to resist pull-out, especially when mounting things on a wall, such as a heavily framed picture, shelves, or cabinets. Ideally, a screw inserted through the finish material fastens directly into a stud. This is not always possible, and anchors are devices which allow the secure mounting of items on a wall between studs.

(1) *Plastic wall anchors* are inserted into predrilled holes in drywall or plaster in order for sheet metal screws to bite into the plastic anchor whose barbs dig into the wall material. They are suited to hanging items weighing less than 50 pounds, and are sold packaged along with screws of compatible size.

(2) *Hollow wall anchors*, also called *molly anchors*, come with a screw already installed. Some can support up to 150 pounds. They have a pointed tip that can be driven into a wall, or must be predrilled. Once in place, the screw is tightened, which squashes and mushrooms out the part of the anchor buried in the wall. The drywall is sandwiched between the deformed anchor inside the wall and a flush metal lip on the outside. The screw can then be backed out or it can be removed entirely.

(3) *Toggle bolts* are used for heavier jobs. Small ones can be used in interior partitions and larger ones used in hollow concrete block. The anchor consists of a metal screw or bolt with a pair of spring-loaded metal wings threaded onto the end. The tip of the anchor is passed through the fixture to be mounted, and is then poked through the skin of the wall into the cavity. When inside, the wings spread out, providing a footing against which the screw can be tightened. It needs to be right first time, though, because the screw has to be removed to take down the project, and once this is done, the wings fall off and will drop to the bottom of the wall cavity.

Screwdriver

Materials: **Wood**
Metal
Masonry
Kits: **All**
Price: **$**
Necessity: **OOOOO**
Skill level: **O**

Screwdrivers were developed once screws were in general use. Before that, the earliest screws were handmade, expensive, and generally used by gunsmiths and clockmakers. The tools used to drive them were makeshift and inconsistent. Oddly, many historical references to screwdrivers, or turnscrews as they were called, involve undertakers. They were the early adopters of the new tools and carried pocket-size screwdrivers to fasten coffin lids at the grave site.

With the blossoming of the Industrial Revolution, screw production became mechanized, a large variety of shapes and sizes of screws became available, especially the simple flathead. It was easy to make and so too were the flat-bladed screwdrivers used to install them.

The *slotted screwdriver,* however, slipped too easily out of the screw's slot in the head, and a blade too small for a screw would twist in the slot, just as a blade too large would not engage in the slot properly. With these flaws in mind, better and varied screw heads were developed.

The first widely used alternative was the *Robertson* or *square-drive screw.* Invented in 1908, these have a slightly tapered square recess in the head. They have been in continuous production since. One of the reasons for the square-drive screw's popularity is that there are only four driver sizes. They engage the screw securely and are less likely to cam out. There are also *combination square-drive/ Phillips™* and *square-drive/flathead screws* that will let you use either type of screwdriver.

In the 1930s automakers were looking for a screw that could be installed by powered screwdrivers. The key requirement was that the driver should slip out of the head and easily disengage or "cam out" of the screw once it was tight. The X-shaped Phillips™ head fulfilled that need and was first used on the 1936 Cadillac.

The Philips™ head screwdriver soon became the most commonly used alternative to the flat-bladed driver, in both hand and machine applications.

The *Torx™ drive*, while a less common drive style, offers improved driving power and grip. Since it is a bit unusual, it's often used on tamper-resistant fasteners.

Choosing a Phillips™ screwdriver with the correct head is crucial. If the tip is too small, it will spin in the head and grind off the edges of the recess, making the screw unusable. If the tip is too big, it will cause damage to both the screwdriver or ream out the recess of the screw head.

One of the best ways to purchase screwdrivers is as a set of a particular drive style, which will provide a range of tip sizes and shaft lengths.

In a set, look for handles that fit well in the hand and will not slip under load. The shank should be made of quality steel. Most shanks are round, but square shanks, which are sometimes found on slotted screwdrivers, provide the option of clamping on an adjustable wrench for additional torque. The longer a screwdriver, the more power you are able to apply to the tip. For tight situations, stubby screwdrivers are available.

Variations:

Jewelers' screwdrivers are used for work on watches and eye glasses. They are held between the thumb and fingertips, with the pointer finger resting on a swiveling pad on the end of the handle, to allow for very fine, precise movements.

Offset screwdrivers are crank-shaped and have a tip on each end. They are used in awkward situations when a straight screw-driver will not fit.

Interchangeable bit screwdrivers have removable, double-ended bits that fit into each end of the shank. The handle is removable and fits on either end. Most have two Phillips™ and two flathead tips—like having four screwdrivers in one.

Screwdriving bits

Materials: **Wood**
Metal
Masonry
Kits: **Apartment**
Home
Price: **$**
Necessity: ○○○
Skill level: ⬡

All of the bits described here are screwdriver-type bit/tips that can be inserted into an electric drill. They do the same job as screwdrivers—instaling fasteners, only faster.

Several different drive styles are available, just as with traditional screwdrivers. Phillips™ bits are the most commonly used, because drywall and deck screws are most often installed by powered drills or screw guns (see page 101). However, slotted, square-drive, and Torx™ bits are also available in a range of sizes to match the screws in use.

Screwdriving bits are divided into two categories, power bits and insert bits, based on how they are held by the drill.

Power bits are designed to be inserted directly into the chuck of the drill. They have hexagonal shafts, so that they can easily be grabbed by the jaws of the chuck. Most are 2 or 3 inches long and often have a *drive* bit on each end. *Extension bits* are just like power bits but are several inches long and will reach into a tight space to drive a screw that cannot be reached with a shorter bit.

Insert bits are small, screwdriving bits, only 1 inch long, and fit into a magnetic bit holder that is chucked into the drill. The simplest bit holder is a magnetic steel sleeve with a shank on the end that fits into the drill chuck. Compared to power bits, these little insert bits are economical to replace when they wear out. They can be used in screw guns and in specialized bit holders for regular electric drills that mimic their action.

Another fastening accessory for the electric drill that is a real time-saver, is the *combination pilot drill and screwdriver*, which uses insert bits. It holds a screwdriving bit on one end, and a drill bit on the other end, and can quickly be flipped over without having to open the chuck. This makes predrilling a hole for a screw (called a pilot hole), and then driving the screw, much faster.

Allen wrench

Materials:	**Metal**
Kits:	**Apartment**
	Home
Price:	**$**
Necessity:	**OOOO**
Skill level:	**O**

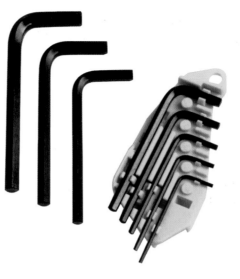

Many fasteners, such as set screws, have a hexagonal recess in their heads rather than the more common pattern indentations that screwdrivers will fit. They are found on bicycles, machinery and ready-to-assemble furniture. An *Allen wrench* is designed to fit into this recess and turn the fastener. It is a precisely sized hexagonal steel bar.

A set screw or bolt with an Allen head has the advantage over other fasteners that the head is more compact and attractive than a standard bolt head. Compared to other types of screws and driving tools, the Allen-style head provides a more secure engagement between tool and fastener.

The simplest Allen wrench is bent to form an L-shape, while other types are straight and have a molded plastic T-handle on one end. Yet others have a six-sided ball milled into the end so that the wrench can be held at an angle to the bolt and still engage the head reliably.

Each type is sold in sets of different sizes. Some sets are packaged loose, while others are hooked onto a key ring. One of the handiest sets groups a variety of sizes into a jackknife-style handle. However, Allen wrenches can be purchased individually in both standard and metric sizes.

Wrench

Materials: Pipes
Metal
Kits: Home
Plumbing
Machine and metal work
Price: $
Necessity: ○○○
Skill level: ○

Wrenches are used to provide a grip on nuts, bolts, and other faceted items when tightening or loosening them.

The simplest are *open-end wrenches*. On each end, there is a C-shaped jaw with parallel faces to fit over square and hex nuts, an advantage when there may be an obstruction above it, and the wrench can be quickly slipped on and off. The jaws differ in size within a set, but the same sizes appear on one end of two different wrenches. This way, a pair of wrenches is available to tighten a matching nut and bolt against each other.

A *box wrench* surrounds the entire perimeter of a nut or bolt head, so it has to slide over the top of the head. While it is less versatile in the amount of access to a nut, the box wrench delivers a more secure grip and has more turning power. With the end of the wrench in a continuous ring, it can be manufactured with thinner jaws than the open-end wrench, giving an advantage where clearance is limited.

The ends of most box wrenches are offset, or bent to the side, so that the handle can clear adjacent obstructions and reach nuts in recessed areas.

The inside of the "box jaw" has either six or 12 faces to grab the corners of the nut. With a six-cornered box, the wrench has to be lifted off the nut and rotated 60° before it can settle back on. A 12-cornered box has to shift only 30°, which again is helpful in tight quarters. The 12-cornered box will also fit over square nuts.

Combination wrenches have one box end and one open end, both the same size. The box end may be slightly offset to position the handle up and away from the work piece.

An *adjustable wrench* is similar in configuration to an open-end wrench, except one side of the jaw can be moved in and out by the turning of a threaded wheel. It makes the wrench weaker than rigid wrenches and does not guarantee a precise fit, but it is very flexible, especially

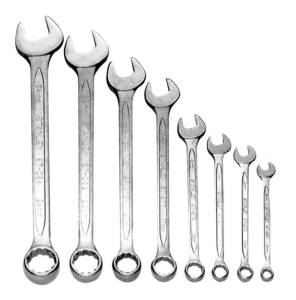

when work is required on standard and metric fasteners. For best results, place the nut as far down between the jaws as possible. Jiggle the wrench a bit to tighten the jaws and ensure they sit properly on the nut. On reapplying the wrench after each turn, check the jaws fit to keep them from loosening and damaging the fastener.

A *monkey wrench* works similarly to the adjustable wrench, although the layout is different and the jaws open wider to accept pipe fittings. The handle turns 90° at the end to form the fixed jaw. The movable jaw slides parallel to it, up and down the handle. A threaded wheel is used to make the adjustments.

The *pipe wrench*, or *Stilson-style wrench*, is the brawniest wrench you are ever likely to own. It is similar to the monkey wrench, but the lower jaw is fixed and the upper, hook-shaped jaw is movable. Its jaws have sharp serrations to dig into and grab smooth pipes and fittings, and as a result, they will *always*

mar the pipe. Pressure has to be applied toward the open side of the jaws for them to grab the work effectively, and they do this so well, in fact, that they can crush thin-walled pipes, such as brass and copper tubing. They should be reserved for heavy iron and steel pipe that will be hidden from view.

Quality wrenches are forged from carbon steel or non-rusting chrome vanadium. They are best purchased in sets which have a range of sizes. Depending on the type of work, you may want to buy both standard and metric sets.

TOP TOOL TIP
It is important to use the right wrench for a fastener. One that is not right can round off the corners of a nut or bolt, making it very difficult to remove. If the fastener is seized in place, soak it liberally with a penetrating oil, such as WD-40™, and let it soak in for a while. It should then be easier to remove.

Socket wrench set

Materials: **Metal**
Kits: **Auto**
Machine and metal work
Price: **$–$$**
Necessity: ⬡⬡⬡⬡
Skill level: ⬡

A *socket wrench set* is a modular system of handles, extensions, adaptors, and sockets. A socket is a steel sleeve designed to slip over a hexagonal nut or bolt head. Inside, the sleeve is shaped like a hexagon or a 12-pointed star. One end is open to fit over the nut, the other end has a square opening that fits over ¼-, ⅜-, or ½-inch square drive stud on the handle. Sockets for each size drive are available to fit a range of standard and metric hard-ware. Adaptors can be used to mix and match handles and sockets.

The basic socket wrench handle is a metal bar with a ratchet mechanism at one end. Several different sizes are available. The ratchet is connected to the drive stud that the socket clips onto. It will turn the socket when the handle is moved in one direction, and "freewheels" when moved in the other direction—like the pedals on a bicycle. The wrench has a flip-lever to decide whether the handle engages for tightening or loosening. This allows the nut to be turned without having to remove the wrench at the end of each turn, and really speeds things up.

Sockets have a few limitations, but most can be overcome. Since the socket must slip over a nut, it cannot reach a nut that is threaded too far down a bolt. For these situations, extra-deep sockets are available. Special sockets used for removing spark plugs are similar to these. When you are unable to get the wrench handle into a confined space, which is common when working on machinery, accessory extension shafts are used to add length between the wrench and the socket. For really tight spots, a universal joint can be added which enables the handle and extension to turn at an angle to the fastener.

Sockets and handles are certainly best purchased as a kit, and several different sizes are available.

Torque wrench

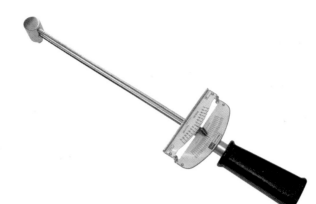

Materials:	**Metal**
Kits:	**Auto**
	Plumbing
Price:	**$–$$$**
Necessity:	**OOO**
Skill level:	**OO**

The *torque wrench* is used to tighten a bolt to a specific pressure. It does so by measuring the amount of twisting force, or torque, that the wrench applies to the bolt. This is necessary when reassembling machinery, as manufacturers will give recommendation on how tightly certain parts need to be fitted. When a component is held on with several bolts, a torque wrench will enable each to be tightened to the determined amount.

There are two styles of torque wrench. The *beam* style is the simpler and cheaper of the two. Two bars are attached to a square drive stud that will hold a socket from a socket wrench. One bar is the handle, and has a grip and a gauge on one end. The other bar is thinner and has a little pointer on the end. The bolt is tightened using the handle, which bends to do so. The thin bar just sits there and stays straight. By comparing the two bars to the gauge, you can see how much the bar with the grip is bending. The gauge is calibrated to show how many feet per pound of torque is applied, based on how much the handle has bent.

The second type of torque wrench is the *clicker* type. A knob on the end of the handle preloads an internal spring to the required torque setting. (Each wrench has a display to indicate the load setting.) As the bolt is tightened, the internal spring holds the drive stud firmly. When the desired torque is reached, the wrench makes an audible "click" as the spring releases and the handle turns freely a few degrees. Then you can move on to the next bolt. The wrench only has to be reset if a different amount of torque is needed. However, it is good practice to unload the wrench before storing it, as leaving it stressed for extended periods can throw off the calibration.

Either type of torque wrench must be handled and stored carefully. Falls and sharp blows can damage its accuracy.

Pliers

Materials:	**Metal**
	Wire and cable
Kits:	**Apartment**
	Home
	Auto
	Electrical
	Machine and metal work
	Craft
Price:	**$**
Necessity:	**⬡⬡⬡⬡⬡**
Skill level:	**⬡**

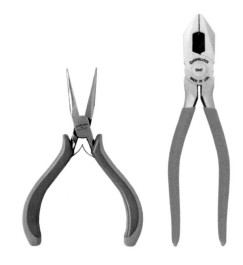

Pliers are used to grasp and hold items that cannot be held in position sufficiently with fingers alone. They are often kept in the same toolbox as wrenches, as they provide an effective backup when the correct wrench is not available.

Pliers open and close in a scissor-like action, but unlike scissors, there are no finger loops to pivot the jaws, and a finger (pinky or ring) must be hooked inside the handle to push them apart. For this reason, it is important that a pair of pliers fits comfortably in the hand. The longer the pliers' handles, the stronger the grip of the jaws. However, if the handles are too far apart to comfortably get the hand around them, it will be difficult to apply a reasonable amount of pressure to firmly hold a nut, bolt, or other item.

Variations:

Many different sizes and styles of pliers have been developed to suit a range of different tasks.

Slip joint pliers are the most commonly used version of the tool. The central pivot point can be set in one of two positions, which changes the distance between the jaws, and enables the pliers to hold a wider range of sizes than they could have otherwise. The jaws are serrated for grip and are flat near their tips for pinching small items, and curved further in for grabbing large items. While pliers are often used to hold a nut or bolt when a wrench is not at hand, care should be taken when doing so. They do not engage the fastener as well as a wrench and the jaws of the pliers can slip and chew up the fastener's edges if not held tightly.

Engineer's or *lineman's pliers* have a single pivot and heavy flat jaws with a pair of diagonal cutters built into them. They are used to pull, twist, bend, and cut wire as well as for general-purpose holding. Their tapered profile slips easily into a tool belt. They are the preferred tool of telephone and electricity linemen, which has led to

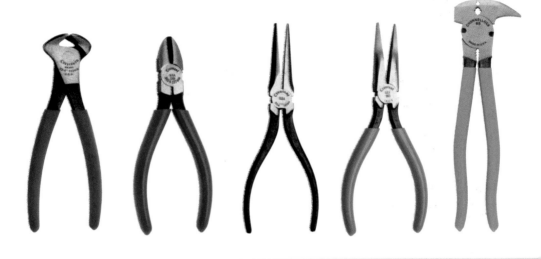

the adoption of the name. Pliers with insulated handles are referred to as *Electrician's pliers*. The precisely aligned jaws can also be used to hold and bend small pieces of sheet metal. The cutters deep in the jaws can withstand the pressure needed to sever thick and tough materials.

Needle-nosed or *long-nosed pliers* are used to reach into tight spaces, to hold small parts or to twist and cut fine wiring. Many have small wire cutters built into the jaws and are used for everything from assembling electronics to removing fishhooks from a catch. Some have tips that are extremely long or that are bent at an angle. Smaller versions have a spring between the handles to assist with opening and closing.

Fence pliers. This is a multi-purpose tool designed for use when instaling and repairing wire fencing and barbed wire. Fence pliers combine several tools in one: the jaws can be used to pull, twist, and splice wire while built-in cutters shear it. A hammer face on one jaw is used to drive staples or nails and a curved claw in the other is used to pull them.

TOP TOOL TIP

Selecting the best size tool is important to avoid damaging the tool or the item being held, and the best choice is a balance of several factors. A set of pliers too big for a job can crush a small work piece and may not reach into a tight spot. Too small, and it is difficult to hold the work securely, causing the pliers to slip and mar the work piece. Squeezing the jaws on pliers on something too hard can bend them, and trying to twist something too stiff can spring the jaws sideways, warping them out of plane.

Tongue-and-groove pliers

Materials:	**Pipes**
	Pipe fittings
Kits:	**Plumbing**
Price:	**$**
Necessity:	**⬡⬡⬡⬡**
Skill level:	**⬡**

Tongue-and-groove pliers are just as handy for grabbing large items as regular pliers are (see page 176). However, their main use is to hold large plumbing fittings that are too big for standard wrenches and where the capacity and holding power of a pipe wrench is not called for.

The long handles of the water pump pliers provide plenty of leverage. The jaws, which may be flat or curved, are adjustable to accommodate items up to several inches in diameter, while remaining parallel to each other. Flat jaws are for grabbing the flats of nuts and plumbing connectors. Pliers with curved jaws are for holding round items.

To handle a range of tasks, the two jaws can slide relative to each other. There are a few mechanisms to lock them into a particular position, and the most reliable is the tongue-and-groove joint, which is a system developed by the Channellock company. As a result, Channellock™ pliers have become a generic name.

Besides plumbing work, they are useful for mundane tasks, such as removing a difficult screw-on cap from a can of finish or a bottle of glue. Also, their curved shape and long handles make them ideal for pulling finish nails from salvaged trim. To do this, grab the nail where it comes out of the back of the piece and roll the pliers to pull the nail through the board, leaving the 'finish' side undamaged.

Locking pliers

Materials: **Metal**
Kits: **Auto**
Plumbing
Machine and metal work
Price: **$**
Necessity: **OOOO**
Skill level: **O**

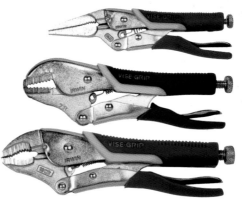

Locking pliers are more readily known by a trade name: Vise grips™. They work like pliers, except that one jaw is adjustable so that the distance between the jaws can be increased or decreased. When set, the handles can be squeezed, locked closed, and will stay closed until a release lever is pressed. They not only grip tenaciously, but they hold themselves in place too. Several versions of the tool have been developed.

The simplest vise grips have serrated, straight or curved jaws that will clamp onto a nut or bolt head. The curved jaws will also clamp around a pipe, for plumbing work. Long-nosed versions will get into small, hard-to-reach spots. Wide, flat "duck bill" jaws are used to clamp and shape sheet metal. Deep C-clamp-shaped jaws with pivoting feet are used for other clamping set-ups.

Locking pliers are versatile, but care should be taken to avoid damaging the work piece. The serrated jaws can easily mar the surface when they clamp down on it. If they happen to slip, they can make a deep scratch, especially when clamped on round objects. If necessary, wrap the work piece to protect it before applying the pliers.

Staple gun

Materials:	**Wood**
	Card
	Fabric
Kits:	**Home**
	Craft
Price:	**$**
Necessity:	**OOOO**
Skill level:	**O**

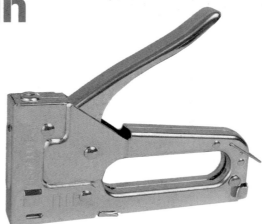

Staple guns are the heavy-duty version of the humble office stapler. They drive thick, stiff staples into a variety of materials, including wood and upholstery, and are handy to have around to tack window screens, tar paper, cardboard, and fabrics into place.

Staple guns use strips of staples that are glued together. Unlike the office version, which uses hand pressure alone, the staple gun has a long, paddle trigger that activates a spring-loaded ram inside the head of the tool. This provides the power needed to staple into dense materials. Older models of the staple gun have a trigger that hinges at the front of the tool, while more recent versions hinge at the rear, which involves applying pressure over the nose where the staples come out, to help counteract any recoil and drive the staple deeper and much more accurately.

If you need to do a lot of stapling, or find it difficult to squeeze the stiff trigger of a manual staple gun, consider using an electric or pneumatic version. These require only a light pull of a trigger in order to activate.

Regardless of the style of stapler you use, be sure to know the brand and model when buying staples. Many companies use a proprietary shape that may or may not be interchangeable with other models.

Adhesive

Materials:	**Wood**
	Plastic
	Card
Kits:	**Apartment**
	Home
	Craft
Price:	**$**
Necessity:	**OOOO**
Skill level:	**O**

There are four types of adhesives designed for use around the house and workshop. Each has its distinctive characteristics, and all are readily available.

PVA glue. PVA stands for polyvinyl acetate, the main ingredient of white and yellow craft and wood glues. It is inexpensive, non-toxic, water-soluble, and easy to clean. Yellow glue is used for woodworking and dries hard, making it easy to sand and less likely to stretch over time. It is not strong enough for structural applications. Some PVA glues are specially formulated to be water- and weather-resistant.

Epoxy glue is a two-part adhesive, consisting of resin and hardener that cures by a chemical reaction when the two are mixed. It is very high strength and will bond dissimilar materials well. While the connection is strong, the trade-off is the limited working time and difficulty of cleaning up any stray material.

Cyanoacrylate. This is the generic name for Krazy Glue™ and similar strong, fast-acting adhesive that bonds wood, metal, ceramics, and some plastics, as well as fingers. It is available in liquid and gel forms, the latter being good for porous materials. Due to its brief cure time, it should only be used for small applications. If you do accidentally glue your fingers, try using acetone-based nail polish remover to release them.

Contact cement is a synthetic, rubber adhesive that requires application to two surfaces, and to be allowed to dry before being joined. A roller is used to apply the cement evenly. Sticks or waxed paper are placed between the parts to be joined so that they can be prior positioned because there is just one chance, as once they touch, they are stuck hard.

SAFETY FIRST
Be sure to read and follow all directions given on adhesive packaging.

Plate joiner

Materials: **Wood**
Price: **$$$–$$$$**
Necessity: **OO**
Skill level: **OO**

The *plate joiner*, or *biscuit joiner*, is used to make a concealed connection when joining the edges of two adjacent boards, such as when building a table top or adding nosing to the edge of a counter. These edges meet at what is known as a butt joint. It is possible to simply glue such edges together, but over time, as wood expands and contracts with fluctuating temperatures, the joint can fail. By adding reinforcement to the joint it no longer need rely solely on the glue.

The invention of the plate joiner in 1955 by the Swiss company Lamello, made this task quick and simple. Rather than use dowels to reinforce joints as was previously done, the new method used small football-shaped pieces of pressed wood which swell when glue is applied. These are referred to as biscuits, because they look like teething biscuits. The plate joiner cuts an arced slot into the edge of a board by plunging a spinning, 4-inch diameter blade into it. Matching slots are

cut on either side of the joint and half the biscuit fits snugly into each.

How far the blade is pushed into the edge determines the depth of the slot and how large a biscuit to be used. All joiners have depth stops that correspond to three standard sizes, 0, 10, and 20—the size number is stamped into the biscuit. Using the correct stop guarantees that the slot is cut to just the right size every time. The tool's adjustable fence helps to locate the cut on the board's edge and keeps the tool square to the work.

Tool manufacturers have continued to develop different versions of the tool with a range of adjustments, body shape, and handle and trigger configurations. Besides being able to cut slots for different size biscuits with the standard blade, some are fitted with a smaller blade, which makes a whole other range of sizes possible. Many tools can also cut slots in angled surfaces, for biscuiting mitered joints.

Doweling jig

Materials: **Wood**
Price: **$**
Necessity: **OOO**
Skill level: **OO**

Before the development of plate joiners (see page 182), to butt-join the edges of a pair of boards and lend strength in the joint, it was necessary to reinforce it with dowels. This naturally can still be achieved. Matching pairs of holes are drilled at intervals down the length of a joint in each of the faces to be joined, and once drilled, glue is applied to the edges and to short, grooved dowels that are then inserted into the holes. The whole lot is clamped up until the glue dries.

In order for everything to line up correctly, the holes have to be drilled just right, which is where the *doweling jig* comes in. The jig clamps to the edge of a board and holds one of several inter-changeable sleeves which are included with the tool. A drill bit is inserted in the sleeve, which is just loose enough to let the bit spin, but tight enough to hold it perfectly perpendicular to the board. Different size sleeves accept different bits, allowing different size dowels to be used.

When the jig is used on both boards to be joined, both holes will line correctly. Two types of jig are available. One auto-matically centers the hole on the edge, while the other type indexes the hole off one face of the board, making it easier to drill off-center holes.

While used less frequently than it once was, the doweling jig is an inexpensive alternative to a plate joiner.

Pop riveter

Materials:	**Sheet metal**
	Plastic
Kits:	**Machine and metal work**
Price:	**$**
Necessity:	**OOO**
Skill level:	**OO**

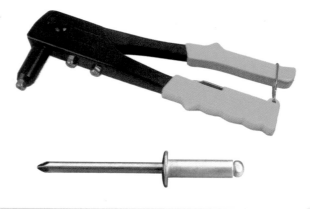

A *pop riveter* is used to fasten together two pieces of thin material, usually sheet metal. Traditionally, rivets were hammered with a ball peen hammer (see page 155), a time-consuming process, and requiring access to both sides of a work piece. The pop riveter is fast and can "blind rivet" from one side of the work.

The rivet is a small aluminum sleeve with a flange on one end. A thin rod with a head on the end, called a mandrel, runs through the center of it. The mandrel slides into an opening in the nose of the pop riveter where it is grabbed by a set of jaws.

The rivet is placed through holes that are predrilled in the sheets. Then the handles of the riveter are closed, like a pair of pliers, and the internal jaws try to pull the mandrel through the sleeve. This spreads and widens it, pinching the sheets between the two ends of the rivet. When the mandrel cannot be pulled any further, the head snaps off with a "pop." The free part of the mandrel is ejected from the riveter and discarded. For added support and resistance to pull-through, a small back-up washer is often placed over the back side of the rivet before it is deformed.

Rivets and a riveter are relatively inexpensive. Good-quality versions have additional tips that can be screwed into the nose to accept different size mandrels.

Hot glue gun

Materials: **Wood**
Fabric
Kits: **Craft**
Price: **$**
Necessity: OOOO
Skill level: O

While adhesives are well suited for high-strength applications, hot melt glue will quickly apply its adhesive to secure materials in a less critical situation. The gun is excellent for craft and hobby work and can be used in the workshop to quickly assemble jigs and mock-ups.

When plugged in, electricity heats a cone-shaped tip on the nose of the gun. Solid sticks of glue are fed through a sleeve in the back of the gun and are forced into the heated tip. Advancing the stick forces melted glue out through the tip and onto the work piece. There it resolidifies and fastens the two pieces together.

The simpler guns require the glue stick to be advanced with the thumb to feed out the melted glue, while glue guns with triggers make this process more comfortable and easy to control. The glue gun draws its heating power from a separate base stand, from where it is removed when being used. The base allows for the detachment of the cumbersome cord during its use.

Glue sticks are available in ¼- and ½-inch diameters. The larger sticks need refilling less frequently and fit into the larger guns.

SAFETY FIRST

The glue gun gets very hot. Not only is the glue hot and capable of burning skin, but it is glue and it will stick to skin until it cools. If you do get some on your finger, wipe it off immediately. Also, note that the gun will remain hot for some time after it has been unplugged. Allow the tool to cool completely before storing it away.

Electric soldering gun

Materials:	**Wire**
	Metal
Kits:	**Machine and metal work**
	Auto
	Electrical
	Plumbing
Price:	**$–$$**
Necessity:	**OOO**
Skill level:	**OO**

Soldering is the process of fusing together two metal parts to provide a mechanical or electrical connection. To make this fusion, a tin/lead alloy with a low melting point called *solder,* is melted and spread over and around the join parts. An *electric soldering gun* provides the heat source necessary to melt the solder and heat the work piece.

The iron has an insulated handle and is held like a pencil. It is heated electrically and remains hot as long as it is plugged in. *Soldering guns* have a pistol-style grip and reach operating temperatures (600 to 800°F) when the trigger is pulled. They may also have a built-in light to illuminate the work.

The small joints that soldering irons and guns are capable of are most frequently used to secure wiring, components, and circuit boards in electronics, or in stained-glass work and jewelry, but large jobs in sheet metal roofing require a substantial iron heated by a gas torch.

When soldering a connection, the pieces must be free from oil and dirt. *Flux* is brushed onto the pieces to remove remaining oxidation which will contaminate the joint. Some solders have a core of flux inside them. The parts to be joined are then heated by holding the tip of the iron to them. When hot, the solder is touched to them, not the iron. The heat of the pieces melts the solder, which flows smoothly around and between them.

There are many different combinations of flux, solder and tool tips that are appropriate for different applications, so it is important to determine which is best for your job. Soldering is a skill and it takes practice to become proficient at it, but the rewards are achieving durable, efficient connections.

SAFETY FIRST
Prolonged heating can damage the tip. The iron should be unplugged when unused for more than 5 minutes or so.

Gas torch

Materials: **Metal**
Kits: **Plumbing**
Price: **$**
Necessity: **OOO**
Skill level: **OO**

Torches are most often used to solder (or sweat) connections on copper water pipes, in order to produce a clean, water-tight connection. They can also be used to thaw pipes, loosen seized bolts, heat plastics for bending, and any tasks that require a high temperature, concentrated heat source.

Simple *gas torches* consist of a steel bottle of compressed flammable gas and a combination valve and tip assembly. Most use propane, which is sufficient for home applications. Several tips are available which will produce different-shaped flames. They have a screw valve that releases the gas when opened, which has to be ignited by a spark from a striker. The flame will light easily if only a small amount of gas is released. More advanced models have a trigger valve that both releases and ignites the gas when pressed. The flame is extinguished when you let go.

Either type of valve should be removed from the bottle when the tool is stored.

SAFETY FIRST
Great care must be taken to shield any flammable materials located nearby when using a gas torch. This is especially the case when carrying out roofing or plumbing repairs, because the torch is often in close proximity to wood framing. Every winter you hear a news story about some yahoo who burned down the house while trying to thaw a pipe. Don't let that be you.

Surface preparation

Surface preparation is either one of the first steps undertaken on a project, or one of the last. When repairing or restoring an item, the first thing to do is to clean it thoroughly to remove any dirt and grime, and corrosion. This makes it easier to disassemble and work on and must be done before applying a new finish. When building from scratch, the final task when applying a finish is to make sure there is a smooth, blemish-free surface. In either case, taking time to prepare will give a far better result in the end.

General rules

• Working carefully with all the tools used throughout the project will lessen the amount of clean-up that needs to be done at the end.

• Fumes given off by strippers or solvents and plastics can be either noxious or flammable, or both. The oils in some exotic woods have been known to cause allergic reactions in some people. Be sure to have a good understanding of the materials you will be working with. Review the manufacturer's labels and take any precautions necessary to proceed safely.

Beginner's class

Sanding is used to fine-tune the surface of a work piece to prepare it to receive a finish, such as paint or polyurethane. Light sanding between coats of a finish is often also required.

1 Coarse abrasives will remove a lot of material quickly on old finishes or to shape a work piece. Progressively finer ones remove less and less material and leave finer and finer scratches until the surface of the work piece is smooth, even and ready for a new finish to be applied.

2 When sanding, take care to remove only enough material to provide a good surface and to soften any sharp edges. Rounding things over too much will affect the appearance of the project and can alter the way that joints fit together.

3 It's important to sand evenly and consistently, as you can create a depression in part of the surface if you concentrate on one spot too long. Using a sanding block will help when sanding large areas. It provides a rigid backup to the sandpaper and ensures that the entire

- When using abrasives, whether sandpaper, steel wool, or polish, work from coarse to fine. Each successive grit erase the scratches left by the previous one

- Don't skip grits. If you jump from very coarse to very fine, you'll have scratches in the finished surface.

- Consider the assembly process before sanding, Some pieces may be easier to sand before the project is put together, others may be easier to do after.

- If you're doing anything that will generate dust, wear a dust mask or respirator.

- When using sandpaper, fold it in both directions before you try to tear it. This will crack the glue and make it easier to tear in a straight line.

- To remove stock quickly when sanding wood, sand at an angle to the grain, then sand parallel to the grain to remove the scratches that result.

- Keep an eye on the abrasive as you work. If it becomes dull or clogged, it won't cut properly and will waste time and energy. Either clean it out, move on to another part the sheet or pad, or replace it with a fresh piece.

- Once you've achieved a smooth surface on a piece of wood that will receive a stain or clear finish, wipe it with a damp cloth and let it dry. The moisture will "raise the grain" and make the surface a bit fuzzy. This fuzz can be easily sanded off. The process makes it less likely that the stain itself will raise the grain and spoil the finish.

surface of the sheet is in contact with the work piece. Rubber sanding blocks are available, but wrapping sandpaper around a flat, rectangular piece of scrap wood works just as well. A sanding block is also good to use on sharp edges as it will prevent the sandpaper from sliding under the grain and lifting a splinter that could jab into your hand.

4 When the sandpaper is held with the hand alone, pressure is placed mainly on the fingertips. This is fine for doing small areas, but it makes sanding large surfaces slower and the results less consistent. When not using a sanding block, use half a sheet of sandpaper that is folded into thirds. This will make a good-size pad that can be refolded to expose a fresh area.

Hand scraper

Materials: Wood
Price: $
Necessity: ●●○
Skill level: ●○

A *hand scraper* is a small, stiff rectangular piece of sheet metal about the size of an index card, sometimes mounted on a handle. It is used to scrape off a fine layer from the surface of a piece of wood, to create a smooth, almost glass-like finish that is hard to beat by any other method. Curved scrapers for finishing contoured surfaces are also available.

The edge of the scraper is square when new and before use it must be "burnished." A hardened-steel burnisher, or the shank of a large drill bit, is held at an angle against the edge and is slid firmly across it. This mashes the edge to create a tiny, hook-shaped burr along its length. It is this sharp little burr that does the work. As the scraper moves across the wood, the burr acts like a small plane blade, slicing off very fine shavings. It is is most efficient on thin or highly figured woods with grain that twists in several directions, because the scraper can shave the surface without digging into the grain.

The scraper is held with both hands and can be pulled or pushed across the work. The trick is to hold it at the correct angle for the burr to cut. A sharp scraper held correctly will make little curls of wood. If you only manage to get dust, try a different angle. Flexing the scraper and angling it across the work piece helps it cut more easily.

Variation:
A *cabinet scraper* is a better tool for the job if there is a lot to do. It has a two-handled frame of wood or metal with which to hold the scraper. A thumbscrew holds it into the frame and flexes it, making the job easier on your hands.

Sandpaper

Materials: **Wood**
Metal
Plastic
Plaster
Drywall
Kits: **Apartment**
Home
Craft
Price: **$**
Necessity: ⬡⬡⬡⬡⬡
Skill level: ⬡

Sandpaper consists of an abrasive that is glued to a backing sheet of paper, plastic or fabric. A number printed on the back of the sheet identifies its coarseness, or grade or grit, which is measured in units between 36 and 600. The higher the number the finer the grit and the smoother the finish. Several types of abrasive and backing materials are used and each has differing characteristics and strengths.

Aluminum oxide is the most common type of sandpaper and is the best choice for preliminary smoothing and shaping of wood. It is brown or gray and ranges in grits from 36 to 220. The advantage of aluminum oxide is that not only is it hard and sharp, but it fragments as it is worked to continually renew the cutting surface.

Silicon oxide sandpaper is usually black and glued on a waterproof backing paper for wet sanding. To wet sand, water is flushed over the surface of a work piece, clearing away dust that can clog the abrasive and prevent heat build-up.

Silicon carbide is very hard but dulls faster than aluminum oxide when worked with wood, as the wood is too soft to break the abrasive away. It is made in very fine grits and is used on metalwork or for sanding finishes between coats.

Garnet sandpaper is red-orange and cuts slower than other abrasives. Because it tends to burnish the surface, it's best for preparing wood prior to finishing. It helps stains absorb into the wood more evenly.

Emery cloth. Black emery abrasive is adhered to a fabric backing making emery cloth flexible and durable. Coarse grits remove paint and corrosion from metal products, and fine grits clean and polish. It is used to prepare copper pipe connections before soldering.

Sanding screens are to sand freshly taped joints in drywall. Comprised of coarse fiberglass mesh covered with abrasive material, drywall dust passes through the screen without clogging. It can be renewed by washing with water.

191

Steel wool

Materials:	**Wood**
	Metal
	Plastic
	Home
Kits:	**Plumbing**
	Machine and metal work
Price:	**$**
Necessity:	⬡⬡⬡⬡
Skill level:	⬡

The now antiquated metal scouring pads once used to scrub pots were comprised of soap impregnated into wads of steel wool. Today, that same steel wool is used in the workshop for scouring, scrubbing, buffing, and polishing.

Steel wool is measured in eight degrees of coarseness, 4 to 1, and 0 to 0000 (the latter pronounced single aught to four aught). Unlike sandpaper, the lower the number, the finer the wool. The size of the wool's steel strands determines how aggressively it cuts. The roughest version can be used to scour away corrosion or remove paint. Pads in the "aught" range are often used to smooth and scuff finishes in between coats. Four aught wool can be used to remove surface rust and polish chrome and other plated metals.

Steel wool should only be used to prepare surfaces for non-water based finishes. The wool tends to pull apart as it is used, leaving fine bits of steel behind. Any left on the surface when the finish is applied will rust. Also, machine oil used in the wool's manufacture can react with the chemicals in water-based coatings, ruining the finish. Non-rusting bronze wool is best for work in damp environments such as boat refinishing.

Variations:
Just as plastic scrubbing pads have largely replaced the steel wool variety in the kitchen, they have also made inroads into the workshop as well. These pads are made of non-woven plastic coated with abrasive. The pad's color denotes the grit. Green is the coarsest, then maroon, then gray. The advantage of the plastic pads is that they don't disintegrate as steel wool does and can be used with water-based finishes. They are good for working on large flat surfaces, but since they are fairly stiff, they can be tough to get into small crevices.

Orbital sander

Materials: **Wood**
Metal
Plastic
Price: **$$**
Necessity: **OOOO**
Skill level: **O**

The *orbital sander* is the simplest and safest of the powered sanders to use. It will perform most of the same type of sanding and finishing work that can be done by hand, but in less time and with less effort.

The sander has a square or rectangular pad at its base to which is clamped a piece of sandpaper. The tool's motor does not spin the pad, but moves it in a very small circle so quickly that the tool feels more like it is vibrating. This "orbital" motion is what gives the tool its name.

There are two types of orbital sander, based on the size of the pad. Larger models require two hands to operate and will hold half a sheet of sandpaper. Smaller models, also called *palm sanders,* hold quarter of a sheet. The large version is good for frequent use and for sanding large areas, while a palm sander is a good choice for lighter, general use. It is compact, and can reach smaller places than the large, half-sheet sander.

For sanding very fine, tight areas, there are *detail sanders*. These are smaller than palm sanders and come in different configurations. Most have a triangular- or teardrop-shaped base that enables the tip of the sander to move into fine corners. Many have interchangeable pads for versatility.

Orbital sanders have one weakness. Their orbiting motion tends to leave tiny swirl marks on the surface of material being sanded, especially with course grit sandpaper. These can be eliminated by using progressively finer grits and then doing a light, final pass over using sandpaper by hand. In situations where this is not an option, a tool known as a *random orbital sander* is useful. It has a built-in mechanism that moves the base pad not in little circles, but in a more random pattern which eliminates marks.

Belt sander

Materials: **Wood**
Metal
Plastic
Price: **$$**
Necessity: **OOO**
Skill level: **OO**

A *belt sander* is a handheld, electric tool that works much like a small benchtop sander (see page 144). The belt sander, however, is portable and can be moved across and around a large work piece to do coarse surfacing and shaping work. A continuous abrasive belt runs over a pair of powered rollers. Between the rollers is a flat piece of metal called the platen that supports the belt during sanding. A pair of handles is attached to a contoured plastic housing covering the motor and the top half of the belt. A D-shaped handle on top of the sander has a locking ON/OFF switch and on the front is a knob to help guide the tool.

It has an aggressive cut and can remove large amounts of material quickly, e.g., to cut the bottom of a door that rubs on the floor, trim molding to fit against a wall or take defects out of the surface of a board.

Floor sanders are basically overgrown belt sanders, with the capability to remove decades of finishes and dents from a wood floor by sanding it down to fresh material ready for finishing.

When using the belt sander, little downward pressure is required. The weight of the tool is usually sufficient. Hold it with both hands and keep moving it around the work piece to prevent sanding a divot in one spot. Position the sander at an angle to the grain to remove a lot of material quickly, or keep it parallel to the grain to minimize scratches that may need to be sanded out afterward.

SAFETY FIRST

It is important to ensure the trigger is in the OFF position before plugging in. Think of the belt as a bulldozer tread with a lot of traction. If the trigger is on when you hit the power, it will take off across the room, scratching everything in its path until it either hits something or yanks the cord out of the wall. Believe it or not, people actually *race* these things! Wear a dust mask because it generates a lot of dust.

Paint scraper

Materials: **Wood**
Kits: **Home**
Price: **$**
Necessity: **ooo**
Skill level: **o**

A *paint scraper* is used to scrape loose and flaking paint from a dry surface or to help remove paint softened with heat or chemical strippers. A wood or plastic handle holds a wide disposable blade with a hooked edge. Short-handled scrapers are intended for use with one hand, while longer-handled scrapers are used with two hands to place additional pressure on the blade for tougher jobs. The better-quality versions have a knob on the back of the tool's head to grab while the other hand grips the handle.

Paint scrapers are useful for removing excess wood glue that had oozed from a joint and dried. Just take care not to scratch up the project in the process.

SAFETY FIRST
Keep in mind that paint, dust, and chips, as well as paint removers, can be a health hazard. If you have to deal with lead paint, call in a professional. For small jobs, be sure to protect yourself and the surrounding area and clean up thoroughly afterward. If using chemical paint stripper, work in a well-ventilated area and follow manufacturer's instructions. To be more environmentally friendly, choose a product that is citrus-based.

Sanding accessories

Materials: Metal
Price: $
Necessity: ●●●
Skill level: ●●

Several accessories are available for rough sanding and scouring using an electric drill. Each of these accessories has a post on the back side that fits easily into the chuck of a drill.

A *sanding disk* is a 4- to 6-inch diameter, rigid plastic disc with a soft rubber face. It is useful for coarse sanding tasks, such as removing paint or rust from metal. Round pieces of sandpaper with peel-and-stick backs (sold in packs at hardware stores and home centers) are adhered to the disc. It will leave swirled scuff marks in the work piece, but these can be lessened by finishing over the area with progressively finer grits of sandpaper. However, some degree of roughness is desirable for a surface that will be primed and painted, as it will help the paint to be absorbed or adhere.

Another tool for scouring away rust and corrosion is the wire brush. The standard *wire brush* is similar to that mounted on a bench grinder (see page 145). Stiff wire bristles spread radially from a center hub. *Cup brushes* have a bundle of stiff bristles held parallel to each other, like a paint brush, and are easier to work across a surface. Both types are available in different sizes and degrees of coarseness.

When using a drill with either accessory, it is usually held with two hands for control—one around the handle, and one around the motor. (Try not to block air vents in the housing.) When the drill is used in this way, it should periodically be allowed to rest and cool. The drill may not be designed for this type of sustained load—for heavy-duty work, use an *electric angle grinder* or dedicated *disc sander* that is built for the task.

SAFETY FIRST
As with all motorized tools, keep loose hair, clothing and jewelry tied back out of the way when using a sander or brush.

Putty and taping knives

Materials: **Wood**
Ceramic
Glass
Kits: **Apartment**
Home
Price: **$**
Necessity: ○○○○○
Skill level: ○

A small, stiff *putty knife* is a simple, versatile tool that should be in everyone's tool kit. The tool was originally used for inserting glazing putty to hold glass in windows. Today it is used to apply all sorts of soft pliable materials, short of peanut butter. It's handy for minor plaster and drywall patching, as well as smoothing and spreading other filler materials. It works for scraping and to open up cracks and small joints. If the edge of the blade begins to round over, use a file to freshen it up.

A *taping knife* is a wide version of a putty knife and tends to be more flexible. It is useful in applying a wide, thin, smooth coating of joint compound or plaster when filling cracks, skimming over a patch or when taping joints where sheets of drywall meet. Taping knives are made in several widths, and two, a 6-inch and a 12-inch width, is good to start with. The wider knife is better when applying the final coats of compound, because the joint is less noticeable if it tapers over a wide area.

A good knife will have a stiff, springy blade and a thick comfortable handle that is securely riveted in place. Some will also have a brass cap on the end of the handle that can be used to tap in drywall nails that may pop loose.

To provide a smooth coat, the knife has to be kept clean. Wash it and dry it thoroughly after use. If residue has dried on the blade, scrape it off, wash the tool and clean the surfaces with steel wool.

Masonry trowel

Materials: **Mortar**
Concrete
Grout
Kits: **Home**
Price: **$**
Necessity: ●●●
Skill level: ●●

A *masonry*, or *brick trowel* is used to apply a bed of mortar and "butter" the ends of bricks when building a brick wall. The most common is the "London" style, which is typically 9 to 12 inches long. The front, or toe, tapers to an acute angle and the heel tapers to a flatter angle. Each edge has a slight curve. A smaller version called a *pointing trowel* is used to repair mortar joints after the wall has been erected.

The *flat trowel* has a single handle mounted in the center of its flat rectangular blade. This is used to float a smooth finish surface onto a concrete slab or mortar bed. Similar wooden trowels are used for the same purpose, but they provide a rougher surface and are used when tile will be laid on top. *Grout trowels* are similar to flat trowels but with a rubber face. They are used to work grout into the joints between ceramic tiles.

TOP TOOL TIP
Brick and masonry work can be a serious undertaking because the work is fairly permanent and mistakes are difficult to remove. It's tough to get a chance to practice. Tile work, which uses masonry trowels, is within the reach of an enthusiastic "do-it-yourselfer," and making a simple tiled tabletop is a good practice project before you decide to tackle your bathroom.

Notched trowel

Materials: **Adhesives**
Kits: **Home**
Price: **$**
Necessity: **OOO**
Skill level: **O**

A *notched trowel* is simply a handle attached to rectangular piece of sheet metal or plastic that has serrations or notches cut into the edge. Trowels are available with notches in different sizes, ranging from ⅟₁₆- to ¼-inch wide .

The trowel is used to spread adhesive, such as the thin set mortar used to hold ceramic tile, or contact cement used to glue down vinyl tile and base. As the adhesive is being spread, a predetermined amount squeezes through the notches and is left on the substrate.

Adhesive designed to be applied in this manner is manufactured specifically to the size of the notches in order to ensure that the correct amount is metered out. The appropriate sized trowel is noted in the instructions on adhesive packaging.

After use, clean the trowel thoroughly, paying particular attention to the notches themselves. If they are clogged or have a build-up of material, they won't distribute the adhesive the next time the tool is used.

Storage and protection

This final section presents items that help to keep yourself, your tools, and your work place in good condition. Also included are some tools that just didn't seem to fit elsewhere. Here too are some tips that relate to safety in the use of tools and equipment.

General rules

- Most safety gear, as well as other items such as ladders and extension cords will bear seals of one or more testing or regulatory agencies. Look for products that have been tested and approved.

- Personal protection gear needs to fit properly. If a device is uncomfortable, distracting or otherwise hindering, seek out an alternative that's better for you.

- While you may be protecting yourself as you work, be aware of any actions you take that may create a hazard for others, such as falling debris, excessive dust, blocked doorways, etc.

- Keep your tools and hardware clean, sharp, and organized. Doing so will make your projects efficient and enjoyable.

Beginner's class

1 Before you can work safely on a ladder, it must first be properly located and erected. Look the ladder over. It should be clean, dry, and undamaged. Moving parts should run freely and function properly. (See more on ladders on page 218.)

2 The ladder should be placed well away from electrical wiring. Aluminum and wet or dirty wood ladders will conduct electricity and pose a shock hazard, so they should never be used near live electricity wires. Fiberglass ladders will not conduct electricity and are therefore the best choice for general purpose.

3 Both step ladders and extension ladders must sit in a solid, level, and dry surface. A stepladder opens to form a self supporting A-shaped structure and when set up, a folding spreader bar connects the two halves to hold them in place. Ensure that it is fully extended and securely locked in position before climbing the ladder. Don't climb a folded stepladder that is leaning against something as it can slip from beneath you

4 When working on a ladder, your body should remain centered between the side rails. If you lean to the side and your navel passes the rail of the ladder, you're leaning too far. The ladder should be

• Keep your work area clean and organized as well. A tangled extension cord run across the floor, a tool left on top of a ladder, excessive sawdust underfoot and other similar scenarios cause accidents.

• Look before you leap. If you have an existing situation to deal with, investigate it thoroughly and understand all the aspects involved before you proceed. The stud finder (page 213) and electrical testers (pages 62 – 3) are designed for specific situations to help you do just that.

• Don't over extend yourself or your equipment. If you need a longer ladder, help with lifting something, a better tool, sleep, etc., stop your work and do so or find another way to do the task. When you force something to work beyond its capabilities, accidents happen.

• Don't bite off more than you can chew. You'll learn things during each project that will prepare you for the next one down the road, but be honest with yourself when assessing whether you have the time, money and skills to take on a particular job.

• Be prepared. Once you've looked over a project and decided that it's within your ability, assemble that tools and materials you'll need before you begin. You maybe won't think of everything, but it will save a lot of running around later. Most of all, be safe and have fun!

---

located so that the area of work will be in front of you and so over-reaching won't be necessary. This may require moving the ladder a few times as work progresses, but it is the safest way to proceed.

5 Straight and extension ladders are designed to lean against something in order to be used. Ideally, they should lean at a 75° angle. Set at a steeper angle, it is more likely to tip over. Set at too shallow an angle, the bottom can slip out from under. Where the ladder leans against the wall,

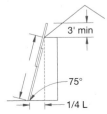

both rails must be well supported. There should be at least 12 inches of solid bearing surface beyond each side of the ladder. Before climbing an extension ladder, ensure that all locking and latching mechanisms are securely engaged.

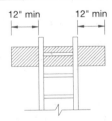

6 To avoid loosing your balance when using a ladder, do not stand above the second to last rung of a step ladder or the fourth to last rung of an extension ladder. Be sure to follow safety instructions printed on your ladder.

Goggles and shield

Materials: **Metal**
Masonry
Wood
Ceramic
Glass
Kits: **Home**
Machine and metal work
Price: **$**
Necessity: **○○○○○**

During many projects, especially ones that involve power tools, there is always the prospect of accidentally getting something in your eye. Even blowing sawdust out of a freshly drilled hole can send a cloud of debris up into your face. To be on the safe side, it's a good idea to wear some sort of eye protection.

Safety glasses are worn to protect against impact. Most have polycarbonate lenses and a UV protective coating. They also have side shields that help prevent debris from getting in around the edges of the lens. *Goggles* also protect against impact and indirectly ventilated or non-ventilated versions will also guard against splashes. All safety glasses and goggles must comply with the ANSI standard Z87.1-1989 and this should be labeled either on the item or its packaging.

Using a *face shield* will help protect the rest of your face against splashes and flying debris. Face shields are considered a secondary line of defense and should be worn along with safety glasses or goggles. A large, clear, flip down shield made from acetate or polycarbonate is attached to an adjustable headgear assembly. A ratcheting or "pin-lock" mechanism is used to adjust the headgear's size to fit. The ratchet style moves by turning a knob on the back and works much quicker, which makes it a better choice for shields that will be worn by several people.

Dust mask and respirator

Materials: **Wood**
Plaster
Drywall
Plastic
Kits: **Home**
Price: **$**
Necessity: **OOOO**

Sawdust is now classified carcinogenic, especially to those exposed to sawdust on a long-term basis. This serves to high-light the importance of ensuring good-quality air is available while working. Many types of potentially harmful dust and fumes are common during demolition, sawing, shaping, sanding and finishing of wood, drywall, and other materials.

Disposable dust masks are going to help when working on light duties. They should fit snugly around their perimeter to avoid any leak which will reduce their effective-ness. Simple paper ones have metal nose clips and a single rubber loop or strap to hold them in place. These are acceptable for nuisance dust only, and offer little protection when spray-painting or from more dangerous dusts, such as asbestos. High-quality masks have stiffer, more restrictive filter materials and better straps, and many have a built-in valve, which makes breathing easier and helps stop glasses from fogging up.

A respirator is a rubber mask that covers the mouth and nose and is held in place with several elastic straps. Attached to the mask is a pair of replaceable cartridges that filter the air as you inhale and a valve that releases air as you exhale. Different types of cartridges are designed to filter out different vapors and particulate sizes. Most varieties sold in home centers and hardware stores are sufficient for the types of dust encountered during building and remodeling. Both respirators and dust masks should be NIOSH (National Institute for Occupational Safety and Health) or OSHA (Occupational Health and Safety Administration) approved.

Hearing protection

Materials:	**Wood**
	Metal
	Masonry
Kits:	**Machine and metal work**
Price:	**$**
Necessity:	**OOOO**

The level of noise can easily be overlooked in the workshop. Guarding against hearing damage may not have the immediacy of the need to protect the eyes or face, but the cumulative effects of noisy power tools can be just as unpleasant and hazardous.

Hearing protection should be worn when around sounds louder than 85 decibels. Since the decibel scale is logarithmic, every increase of 10 dB will make sounds seem twice as loud. An electric drill runs around 88 dB, table saws range between 90 and 100 dB and routers average around 100 dB.

Items that are designed to muffle sound have a noise protection rating or NPR, which is the number of decibels by which the ambient sound is reduced. *Padded earmuffs* have an NPR of 15 to 33, depending on type. These are large, hard-shell muffs connected with a wide headband that fit over the head like a pair of old-fashioned headphones. Earmuffs can be cumbersome to wear with goggles and a face shield, but they are quickly removed. *Disposable foam earplugs* reduce sound by around 33 dB. These little foam plugs are squeezed and inserted into the ear where they expand. They are comfortable, although they take a few seconds to seat themselves in the ear. *Hearing bands* have an NPR of 21 to 28 and look more like Walkman™ headphones. They have rubber plugs tot fit into the ear. These combine the features of the ear plugs and muffs but at a reduced NPR.

NPR is determined under controlled laboratory conditions, but the real world just isn't that precise. In practice, the actual noise reduction provided by these devices is less than is stated by the NPR rating. Most will offer significant reduction however and should not be disregarded.

Body protection

Materials: **Head**
Hands
Feet
Back
Kits: **Apartment**
Home
Price: **$**
Necessity: **OO**

Hands, feet, and torso need protection against impact and chemicals.

Gloves. Cotton gloves are the simplest and the best for light yard work, although they can prove to be slippery on some tool handles. Because of this, some makes will have the fingers and palms rubberized to aid grip. Leather gloves are by far better when engaged in demolition work. Deerskin is more flexible, but calfskin is cheaper and tougher. Tougher work gloves use high-tech materials, are reinforced at points that get a lot of wear, sometimes insulated against the cold, or may incorporate a layer of vibration damp-ening material to lessen the effects of long-term vibration. Special puncture resistant gloves are covered with fine mesh to protect your hands if a knife, chisel or gouge accidentally slips. Disposable latex and vinyl gloves keep hands clean when using water-based finishes, but not from absorbing the chemicals in oil or lacquer-based finishes. Nitrile gloves do protect against these and most solvents.

Back support braces are made of an elastic fabric with internal ribs and are held in place around the torso with Velcro™. They function like a weight-lifting belt to help protect the back when lifting heavy objects.

Knee pads make jobs like instaling floors, painting baseboards, or setting patio pavers more comfortable. Lightweight foam pads are available, but tougher ones with rubber or hard plastic caps over internal padding offer more support and protection.

Footwear. Sturdy shoes or boots with good arch support will tire your feet less at the end of the day. Soles need deep treads made from an oil-resistant material to minimize slipping. Ankle-high boots provide good support, though low-cut shoes are more comfortable when squatting or kneeling. Safety shoes and boots have a steel or composite plastic cap built into the toe to protect against crushing.

Toolbox

Materials: **Tools**
Kits: **Apartment**
Home
Plumbing
Electrical
Auto
Price: **$–$$$**
Necessity: **⬡⬡⬡⬡⬡**

The earliest toolboxes were little more than utilitarian shipping containers. Today, this may be the case for a few professional woodworkers, but for amateurs, simple, mass-produced tool totes are the norm. The most utilitarian is the 5-gallon bucket that paint and joint compound is supplied in. These are commonly discarded on construction sites and have been adopted as expedient (and gratis) tool carriers. Nylon covers with compartments and pockets are manufacturered to slip over the rim to keep things organized. *Hardware trays and pouches* are also designed to stack inside these buckets.

More "traditional" toolboxes are made of plastic and steel. Plastic is lighter, steel is more secure.

Large, steel, static tool chests, known as mechanic's tool chests, are designed to house machine tools, such as sockets, taps, wrenches, etc. Most feature several shallow, slide-out trays that allow tools to be accessed at a glance.

Parts drawers. Projects are a lot less fun if you are constantly searching for the right nails, screws, bolts, and other fasteners. Dumping them all in an old coffee can doesn't cut it. A set of parts drawers is a fine way to keep things organized. They are small cabinets that hold 20 or 30 clear plastic drawers, and a great way to sort and group.

Extension cord

Materials: **Power tools**
Kits: **Home**
Price: **$–$$**
Necessity: **OOOO**
Skill level: **O**

Drawing power through an *extension cord* is like sucking a milkshake through a straw. The same is true for the wire in an extension cord. The electricity used to power a tool must travel from the wall outlet, through the wiring within the cord, to the tool. Whenever electricity travels through a wire, it encounters resistance. The smaller the wire, the more resistance there is. Also, the longer the wire, the more resistance there is as the electricity travels from one end to the other. There is more electricity at the end of a short, fat wire than at the end of a long, thin wire. If a power tool cannot receive the power it needs, its performance will be diminished. At worst, long-term, under-powered use will destroy the motor. For best results, use cord with thick wiring that is no longer than is necessary.

A wire's thickness is called gauge. The lower the gauge number the thicker the wire. For use with power tools, the gauge should be no more than 16; 14 gauge is sufficient for most cords up to 50 feet long; 12 gauge is best for cords 100 feet long.

The insulation on a cord needs to be thick for durability, but always check the gauge printed on the side, as it could be thin wire surrounded by lots of insulation. You should also look for the regulatory bodies' labels to indicate the cord meets correct standards of manufacture. All cords and the tools that are plugged into them should be correctly ground. The plug should be molded and fully reinforced onto the cord or fully reinforced.

SAFETY FIRST
Harsh use can abrade the cord and lead to a short. The cord should not be closed in doors or pulled over sharp corners. Never pull the plug from the wall by yanking the cord; always grab the plug itself. When coiling up for storage, gather it loosely in loops, rather than in tight twists around your thumb and elbow.

Ladder

Kits: **Home**
Price: **$$**
Necessity: **OOO**
Skill level: **O**

Ladders are designed for different uses.

Step stools have one step and can be stood full upon. *Step stand*s have several steps, with a platform at the top on which it is safe to stand. Many step stands have a frame that extends above the platform, which is used to steady yourself against.

Stepladders are folding steps that are A-shaped in stance when open and erected for use. They range in size from 6 to 12 feet high and often have a folding platform near the top to hold tools or a paint can. Unlike step stands, it is unsafe to stand on this top platform.

Extension ladders are a pair of straight ladders that slide along each other's length. They are extended by using a rope and pulley to adjust the height, from 20 to 40 feet depending on the model.

Combination ladders are similar to stepladders although they have additional hinged joints halfway up each side. Three joints are able to lock in several positions, making them very versatile. A combination ladder can be configured as a stepladder, a straight ladder, as a horizontal scaffold and can be folded so that it will rest evenly on a stairway. They are made from aluminum, wood, or fiberglass. Fiberglass is light, strong and non-conductive, a good choice when working near electricity cables. Aluminum is strong and light. Wood is often the least expensive option and is non-conductive when clean and dry.

Ladders have load ratings to measure the weight they can hold. Light household ladders take up to 200 pounds. A sturdier model suitable for medium- or heavy-duty, will handle 225 or 250 pounds respectively.

SAFETY FIRST

Look for regulatory approval stickers, to indicate the ladder has met the required standards of construction. Read the safety instructions on a ladder before use—it can be dangerous to use ladders that are not correctly set.

Drain auger

Materials:	**Plumbing**
Kits:	**Plumbing**
Price:	**$–$$**
Necessity:	**OOO**
Skill level:	**OO**

When a plumbing clog in a drain or wastepipe cannot be cleared with a plunger or drain cleaner, the *drain auger* is the next line of attack. The auger, also called a snake, consists of a long, flexible shaft with a sharp spiral hook on the end. This is fed into the drain line through the toilet, the mouth of the drain, or through a clean-out opening in the waste line. The auger is turned as it is fed in, to break up any obstructions as it progresses, and these are then pulled out with the auger when it is removed.

Varieties vary in the length of the shaft and the means by which the auger is turned. The simplest is about 25 feet long and is turned by hand using a built-in crank. A more specialized variety is known as a toilet or closet auger. It measures about 3 feet long and is used specifically for toilet clog-ups. It has an extra long handle with a vinyl or rubber clad elbow at the end to protect the bowl when the auger is in use.

An electric drill can be used to power stronger drain augers. Some have drills that are built-in while others can be attached to an electric drill. All augers have a housing that stores and protects the auger when coiled up and not in use.

SAFETY FIRST
Wear rubber gloves when dealing with drains, and thoroughly clean the auger after use.

209

Sharpening stone

Materials: **Chisels**
Knives
Plane irons
Kits: **Home**
Price: **$**
Necessity: **OOO**
Skill level: **OO**

Tools such as chisels, knives and planes need to be properly sharpened to work safer, more enjoyably and efficiently. When a cutting tool is sharp, its two cutting edges are completely flat and meet at a perfect line. This allows the tool to cleanly slice its way through the material to be cut. As the tool dulls, the perfect line will round over into a blunt wedge and lose its effectiveness. To resharpen this line, the surfaces of the tool are ground back to their original shape.

Sharpening stones are blocks of abrasive for grinding cutting edges back into sharpness—a process called honing. There are three types of stones for honing and each is available in a range of different grits. *Oilstones* and *waterstones* may be natural or man-made and use oil or water to carry away metal filings and lubricate the tool as it is honed. Waterstones make honing faster, while oilstones are easier to maintain and set up. *Diamond hones* are man-made and have industrial diamond

dust embedded in their surface. They sharpen blades quickly, but they are a more expensive product.

To sharpen an edge, the cutting tool needs to be held at the correct angle to match the one already ground on the tool (typically between 25 and 35°). The use of a *sharpening jig* makes achieving this angle a lot easier. It's a small holder with wheels on the bottom that the tool is clamped into. As you roll it back and forth across the stone, the tool is thereby held at the correct angle throughout the sharpening process.

Entire books have been dedicated to tool-sharpening methods. If you plan to work a great deal with chisels, knives, or planes, you will need to sharpen the tools regularly and acquiring a good reference book is to be recommended.

Caulk gun

Materials:	Wood
	Plastic
	Ceramic
Kits:	Home
Price:	$
Necessity:	OOOO
Skill level:	OO

Caulk is used to seal and waterproof interior and exterior joints and to close small gaps prior to painting. The most common caulking task a home owner will do is to repair the surrounds of a shower cubicle or bath tub. While caulk is available in small toothpaste-size tubes from which it can be applied, it is also sold in larger quantities in rigid paper or plastic tubes that require a dispensing *caulk gun*.

The gun consists of a frame that holds the tube, and a pistol handle with a wide trigger that advances a plunger. A release button on the side of the handle allows the plunger to be pulled all the way back so the tube can be loaded.

Before the tube can be used, the tip of the nozzle is trimmed off at an angle and a membrane seal at its base is broken. Once the tube is in the frame, the plunger is advanced into the bottom of the tube. Squeezing the trigger will force the caulk out of the tube onto the work piece. To stop the flow, the release button on the side of the handle is pressed. If there is caulk left in the tube when the job is done, the tip can be sealed to prevent the caulk from drying inside and rendering the rest of the tube unusable.

Inexpensive caulk guns have thin, stamped sheet metal frames. Better-quality ones have cast metal components, a smoother operation and some additional features, such as a tip cutter within the handle or a built-in rod for breaking the membrane seal.

Wet/dry vacuum

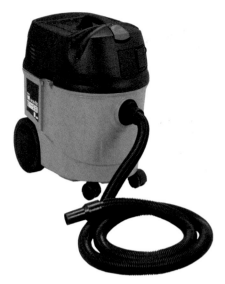

Materials:	**Wood**
	Metal
	Water
Kits:	**Home**
Price:	**$$**
Necessity:	**OOOO**
Skill level:	**O**

If you are planning a workshop, or intend to undertake a fair amount of renovation work, a small *wet/dry vacuum*, also known as a shop vac, is a worthwhile investment. A shop vac is a large canister vacuum cleaner with a wide hose that can suck up just about anything. It's indispensable for cleaning up a work area after a project.

The interesting thing about their design is that none of the debris passes through an impeller or other mechanism. It is simply drawn into the canister where it falls to the bottom. The top of the vacuum, which holds the motor and filter assembly, can be lifted off, allowing the contents of the canister to be removed and dumped into a garbage bag.

Since the motor is isolated from the debris stream, the vacuum can also be used to clean up water from a spill or leak. The water collects in the canister and can be drained out later.

Several sizes of wet/dry vacs are available. While you best buy one large enough to suit your needs, don't get one that's too large unless you have room to store it. Like all vacuums, a shop vac will have a set of attachments; brushes, crevice tools, and squeegies. On most models, the only replaceable part is the filter, which must be cleaned or discarded when clogged.

Stud finder

Materials: **Walls**
Kits: **Home**
Price: **$**
Necessity: **OOOO**
Skill level: **O**

When hanging something heavy on a wall, the best option is to anchor the item directly into a wall stud. Studs are the vertical wood or metal framing members behind a wall facing. The trick is finding them behind the drywall or plaster.

A stud finder is like a small handheld sonar machine. Hold the ON button and slide it across the wall surface, and the finder scans for changes in density. As it comes to the edge of a stud, a series of lights turn on and an audible signal is given. When it passes the other edge of the stud, the signal stops and the lights go out. The edges of the stud can then be marked with pencil and the fastener located between the two pencil marks.

There are several different models with a variety of features. Some have dual scanning depth detectors, which makes the tool useful for plaster as well as thinner sheetrock walls. Some can scan even deeper to find pipes and yet others can sense live wires in the wall, allowing you to trace wiring which is helpful in avoiding drilling or screwing into a cable.

Studs are generally located 16 inches on center, so once you find one, odds are you'll find another 16 inches away. Doubled studs are located either side of door and window openings and at the corners of a room. Outlet boxes are usually attached to the side of a stud.

Knocking on the wall can also roughly indicate where a stud is. The sound is more hollow between the studs. Another trick is to put your cheek against the wall and shine a flashlight along its surface. Look for vertical waves in the surface and popped nail or screw heads, to indicate joints in the drywall that have been positioned over a stud.

Glossary of terms

Bevel A type of cut where the saw or blade is tipped to the side to cut an angled path down through the work piece.

Collet A clamping device commonly used on routers that is similar to a chuck and used to hold a bit into a tool.

Cross cut In wood, a cut made across the grain. In other materials, a cut made across the width of the work piece.

Cut-out The sheet or block of waste material that is the result when a large hole is cut or sawn from a work piece.

Dado A long groove cut into the surface of a work piece.

Down-stroke The down-ward motion of a tool or cutting edge.

End grain The condition where a cut has been made across the grain of the wood and the severed ends are exposed. Usually visible at two ends of the board.

Fence A long, straight edge used to guide material through a tool parallel to a blade or cutting bit.

Formwork A temporary structure that acts as a mold for poured concrete and is removed once the concrete has cured.

Flux A solution applied to a joint prior to soldering, used to help the solder flow and to remove impurities that may compromise the strength of the connection.

Grain The long, parallel tubes that make up a piece of wood.

Ground In order for an electrical circuit to function properly, it must have a direct or indirect connection to earth. This connection is called the ground.

Hardwood Dense wood, usually from deciduous trees such as oak, maple, cherry, and ash.

Heft Weight or substance.

Kerf The gap in a work piece created by a saw

blade as material is sawn and removed during the cutting process.

Knot A hard formation occurring at the point a branch intersects a tree trunk.

Miter A type of cut where the saw or blade is turned to the left or right to cut an angled path across the work piece.

Millwork Trim work such as baseboards, door frames, windowsills, etc.

Molding A shaped outline or profile used on wood cornices as decoration.

Mortise A pocket shape cut into a work piece, usually rectangular, and sized to receive a tenon, a hinge or lock.

Off-cut A piece of scrap material that results when a work piece is cut to size.

Plumb An object that is truly vertical in all directions. To verify this is to "check for plumb."

Rabbet A long groove cut out of the edge of a board so that a lip remains along the board's length. The lip can fit into a matching groove made in another work piece to join the two.

Rip saw In wood, a cut made parallel to the grain. In other materials, a cut made along the length of the work piece.

Softwood Wood from a coniferous tree, such as spruce, pine or fir. It generally less dense and easier to work than wood from deciduous trees.

Shoring Temporary supports or bracing that can be erected during a construction project.

Shim Thin or wedge-shaped pieces of material placed between two or more objects to precisely adjust their position relative to one another. Also used as a verb: to position by use of shims.

Square Items that are square are positioned at 90° to one another. Also used as a verb: to position two items at 90° to one another.

Straightedge Any truly straight edge, such as a ruler or square, that can be used as a reference or to guide a tool, such as a utility or hobby knife, or a marking instrument.

Tenon A round or rectangular tab cut into a work piece that is sized to fit a matching pocket (mortise) in a second piece.

Turning The process of making something on a lathe. An item made on a lathe is said to have been turned.

Swarf The filings or shavings that result from using a file, rasp, or sandpaper.

Tang The tapered end of a file or chisel over which the handle fits.

TPI The coarseness of a saw or saw blade is measured by the number of teeth it has per inch of length.

Resources

Surfing the Web is a good way to review and compare the variety of manufacturers. While not exhaustive, this list provides links to some of the major players in the field.

Power Tools
Black & Decker *www.blackanddecker.com*
Bosch *www.boschtools.com*
Dremel *www.dremel.com*
Delta *www.deltawoodworking.com*
DeWalt *www.dewalt.com*
Jet *www.wmhtoolgroup.com*
Makita *www.makita.com*
Milwaukee *www.milwaukeetool.com*
Porter Cable *www.porter-cable.com*
Powermatic *www.wmhtoolgroup.com*

Hand Tools
Adjustable Clamp Company
 www.adjustableclamp.com
Bessey Clamps *www.jamesmorton.com*
Channellock *www.channellock.com*
Cooper Hand Tools
 www.cooperhandtools.com
Estwing *www.estwing.com*
Irwin *www.irwin.com*
Klein Hand Tools *www.kleintools.com*
Lie-Nielsen *www.lie-nielsen.com*
Stanley *www.stanleyworks.com*

There are websites to be found that are the online presence of catalog, mail order, and bricks and mortar retailers. Each sells tools, but tend to specialize in a particular area. Some sell a variety of inexpensive imported tools; others focus on high-end hand tools. In addition, many sell hard-to-find hardware, materials, and supplies, as well as related books and videos. Their catalogs are a good source of information not only about particular tools, but about materials or projects too.

Ace Hardware Stores
 www.acehardware.com
Duluth Trading Co. *www.duluthtrading.com*
Eastwood *www.eastwood.com*
Garrett Wade *www.garrettwade.com*
Harbor Freight *www.harborfreight.com*
Hartville tool *www.hartvilletool.com*
Lee Valley *www.leevalley.com*
The Japan Woodworker
 www.japanwoodworker.com
McFeely's *www.mcfeelys.com*
McMaster Carr *www.mcmaster.com*
True Value Hardware Stores
 www.truevalue.com
Rockler *www.rockler.com*
Sears Craftsman
 www.sears.com/craftsman
Woodcraft *www.woodcraft.com*
Woodworker's Supply
 www.woodworker.com

Acknowledgments

Thanks go to my parents, to my wife Ji, to the Dodds and Wanapun families, and to Sid.

The publishers would like to thank the manufacturers who provided many of the photographs:

Adjustable Clamp Company
Black & Decker
Bosch
Channellock
Cooper Hand Tools
Delta Machinery
DeWalt
Dremel
Irwin Industrial Tools
Makita Industrial Power Tools
Milwaukee Electric Tool Corporation
James Morton Ltd
Porter-Cable
Stanley Sales Ltd

Other photography
Keith Waterton—pages 2, 10, 13, 14, 17, 18, 24 to 39, 40, 44/5, 72, 98, 181, 191, 200, 205, 208.

Steve Dodds—pages 51, 52, 54, 62, 63, 67, 75, 77, 95, 99, 107, 114, 116, 121, 123, 126, 132, 133, 143, 147, 151, 156, 160, 161, 164, 165, 167, 175, 183, 187, 196, 198, 199, 201, 202, 204, 207, 211, 213.

All the sketches were produced by Steve Dodds.

The publishers would also like to thank the staff, especially Kevin Draper and Bob Overall at Gibbs and Dandy, St Ives, Cambridgeshire for their assistance; staff at Homebase Ltd, Cambridgeshire; and Tim Archer of St Ives, Cambridgeshire for use of his workshop for photography.

Index